Speaking of Mother Earth

John H. McMurphy

Harriet Kofalk

Amy Martin

Jeff Davis

Amaranth Publishing

Speaking of Mother Earth

Published by:

Amaranth Publishing
P.O. Box 764167
Dallas, TX 75376

ISBN 0-9635487-7-8

Cover Art created by John Nicholas of Composite Color, Ltd. in Dallas

For information on "Speaking of Mother Earth" workshops, please call toll-free in the U. S. & Canada: (800) 321-2760

— Printed on Enviro-Text, a recycled book paper —

Dedication

The Earth is Mother of all that is natural.

She is Mother of all,
for contained within her
are the seeds of all.

She is in so many ways fruitful.
All creation comes from her depths.

Hildegard of Bingen

. . .

Since the dawn of modern human consciousness more than 35,000 years ago, intimacy with Mother Earth's creativeness has been the primary inspiration for humanity's creativeness. Our intimacy with her natural rhythms and beauty has stimulated our imagination and has enriched our experience of life. Many people of the world remain intimate with Mother Earth, a relationship demonstrated by their harmonious lifestyle.

Even in Western cultures that have forgotten their bonds with Mother Earth, she still has a voice among writers, artists, mystics, and scientists who hold dialogues with her creativeness. Beethoven, O'Keeffe, Thoreau, Wordsworth, St. Francis, da Vinci, and Hildegard of Bingen are but a few whose intimacy with Mother Earth stimulated their imaginations and their creative endeavors.

We who have created this book have drawn upon our own relationships with Mother Earth's creativeness for our inspiration. We dedicate our fruits to her. *She is in so many ways fruitful.*

TABLE OF CONTENTS

PART ONE
Our Mother Earth Heritage

Consider the following thoughts about Mother Earth for a moment before you begin this section:

God manifests through everything...all is Divinity and Nature herself is the body of God.

Ernest Holmes, *The Science of Mind*

The lover of nature is...one who learns from nature the lesson of worship.

Ralph Waldo Emerson, *Nature*

For prehistoric people, nature was not just a treasure-trove of "natural resources." Nature was a goddess, "Mother Earth,"...The whole environment was divine.

Arnold Toynbee

The earth is a living being who has a soul...It is a spiritual being.

Plato, *Timaeus*

Mother Earth, her life am I
Mother Earth, her body is my body
Mother Earth, her thoughts are my thoughts.

Navajo Song

This earth which is spread like a map around me is the lining of my inmost soul exposed.

Henry Thoreau, *Journals*

Everything that is in the heavens, on the earth, and under the earth is penetrated with connectedness, penetrated with relatedness.

Hildegard of Bingen

The earth whose heart is in the highest heaven; immortal, surrounded by truth... Oh, Mother Earth!

Athara Veda (Ancient spiritual text from India)

Wondrous truths, and manifold as wondrous,
God hath written in those stars above;
But not less in the bright flowerlets under us.

Henry Wadsworth Longfellow, "Flowers"

.   .   .

Reverence for Mother Earth is the foundation for our spiritual awareness from prehistoric cave art to such diverse spiritual practices as Native American traditions, Taoism, Transcendentalism, Hinduism, Judaism, and Christianity. The ideas and prayers above reflect the widespread awareness that Mother Earth is sacred; she is the symbolic body of God.

Mother Earth is the physical manifestation of the Divine Creative Intelligence we often call "God." Each of her life–creating and life–sustaining processes are Divine Intelligence in operation. To know God, says Emerson, we need only to look around us to Nature. Most people in Western Civilization today, however, have forgotten Mother Earth's sacredness.

Our amnesia is no accident. Church historians have documented Western culture's ancient practice of and later abandonment of Mother Earth spiritual traditions. Historic evidence indicates that both Judaism and Christianity actually evolved from Mother Earth consciousness. In fact, many Judeo–Christian spiritual themes, holidays, and celebrations are "Judeo–Christianized" versions of ancient Mother Earth spiritual themes, holidays, and celebrations.

Mediterranean
Anima Mundi
& sacred chalice

Since prehistoric times, the Mediterranean and Near East were strongholds of Mother Earth religions. Both Judaism and Christianity began in these regions as relatively minor religious movements surrounded by powerful Mother Earth religions. Believing that there is safety in numbers, Jewish and Christian leaders determined that, in order to survive amidst these other religions, they needed to increase their audience.

As Mother Earth beliefs, holidays, and festivals were quite popular, Jewish and Christian leaders needed strategies to sway people away from Mother Earth traditions into their practices and to create greater acceptance for their new traditions within the community. Part one of their strategy was to create a drawing card to attract people and to enhance their acceptance.

Imagine that a new health and fitness club opens in your neighborhood. The owners, knowing that three other fitness clubs already exist in the area, want to attract you and your neighbors who may be members of these other clubs and who are familiar with the benefits of regular exercise. As a drawing card, they offer their targeted clientele free trial memberships or free fitness testing.

Jewish leaders used a similar strategy in ancient times to establish their presence as a viable religion in the Near East, as did early Christian leaders in the first few centuries after the life of Jesus. These new religions adopted into their own spiritual framework several Mother Earth practices and rituals, including the following examples:

- Passover was originally an ancient Canaanite (a Mother Earth tradition) ritual practiced by shepherds on the night of the full moon at the Spring Equinox. The earlier Canaanite ritual, according to the *Encyclopedia of Theology*, has essentially the same theme and message as Passover which later subsumed it.

- Solomon's Temple in Jerusalem was not inspired by spiritual wisdom unique to the Hebrew people; instead, it was inspired by ancient Syrian temples which were built about two thousand years earlier than the Temple in Jerusalem.

  The World Atlas of Archaeology reveals that recent Near East excavations show Solomon's Temple is directly linked to earlier Syrian temples which contained significant Mother Earth design themes. Like most Mother Earth sacred sites in Syria and in other places, Solomon's Temple was built with a Spring Equinox orientation. At dawn on the Equinox—one of the most important holy days in Mother Earth religions—a beam of sunlight entered the Temple doorway, passed over the altar, and fell upon the Holy of Holies. Only on this day would the priest enter the Holy of Holies.

• Easter honors the re–birth of Jesus after his death just as world Spring Equinox festivals honor Mother Earth's re–birth from the "dead" of winter (the Greek myth of Demeter and Persephone is one example). The date for Easter—the first Sunday after the full moon of the Spring Equinox—still is determined by the Mother Earth festival it later absorbed.

• For other examples, please see the Mother Earth Sacred Calendar.

Once people familiar with the Mother Earth traditions found these new religions could satisfy their genuine need to celebrate their spiritual beliefs through ritual and festivals, a few left their old ways and began to practice the new traditions. Many others who remained faithful to their Mother Earth religions began to accept the new religions as worthwhile additions to the spiritual life of their communities.

Eventually, Judaism and Christianity in their respective time periods had adopted many Mother Earth principles and practices and made them significant elements of their own religious perspective. Once these new religions' presence was firmly established as members of the spiritual community, Jewish and Christian leaders unveiled part two of their strategies.

The next step both these new religions took was to discourage people from worshipping according to their Mother Earth heritage. At first Jewish and Christian leaders merely issued warnings to their flocks about continuing the old ways. When warnings failed to stop the popular worship activities and festivals, leaders set punishments, some quite severe, for those who continued the ancient religious practices. Yet, most people still worshipped Mother Earth as sacred.

Finally, leaders resorted to violence to solve their problem. People who still practiced the old ways were declared to be enemies of the new religions. Their sacred sites and temples were destroyed, and their sacred texts burned. Mother Earth had become *persona non grata* in the spiritual community.

Some brave souls who were committed to their ancient ways went to their death. Others went into hiding and secretly practiced their Mother Earth traditions. History shows that the prejudice and violence directed toward religions which see Mother Earth as sacred continued during the European conquest of the Americas, Africa, India, and Oceania. It is still with us.

Healing the wounds, hearing the voice

Some people today are angry and blame Judaism and Christianity for these injustices. Blaming those whose intolerance and prejudice has caused suffering does not change what has happened, nor does it diminish the pain. It only generates more anger and animosity in a world that certainly lacks neither. If we desire a spiritual relationship between ourselves and Mother Earth, then we need healing and love—not blaming and anger.

Contemporary spiritual thinkers such as Louise Hay, Gary Zukav, and Shakti Gawain advise us that genuine healing begins when we accept *what is*—not what we wish to be or wish to have been. Major Western religions have been and continue to be prejudiced against Mother Earth as the sacred embodiment of God. That is *what is.*

We must accept that Western civilization does have within its belief structure a prejudice against Mother Earth and the people who see her as sacred. We also must accept that we who are "products" of Western culture—even if we do not consciously demonstrate prejudice toward Mother Earth—may unconsciously harbor effects of our culture's prejudices. *Owning* this part of our collective psyche is an important step in the healing process.

We must not forget, however, that also within our psyche is the capacity for experiencing Mother Earth as sacred, as the symbolic embodiment of God. Consider for a moment the following passages from Western mystics, artists, poets, and musicians.

Earth, with her thousand voices, praises God.

Samuel Taylor Coleridge, "Hymn Before Sunrise"

The day of my spiritual awakening was the day I saw—and knew that I saw—God in all things.

St. Matilda

When I stand alone with the earth, a feeling of something in me going off in every direction into the unknown of infinity means more to me than anything organized religion gives me.

Georgia O'Keeffe, *Letters*

The natural world is a spiritual house...
Man walks there through forests of physical
    things that are also spiritual things,
That watch him with affectionate looks.

Charles Baudelaire, "Intimate Associations"

I get my ideas amid the freedom of Nature, in the woods, on walks.

Beethoven

To him who in the love of Nature holds
Communion with her visible forms,
She speaks a various language.

William Cullen Bryant, "Thanatopsis"

•   •   •

Mother Earth still has a voice within the Western psyche. It may be faint or difficult to distinguish amid the myriad other voices we hear—but she is there! Our artists, poets, musicians, and mystics hear her voice and comprehend her unique language. They respond with verse, songs, images, and other testaments to their spiritual relationship with Mother Earth and the Divine Reality she embodies.

Maybe you do not consider yourself an artist, poet, or mystic. That does not matter. You probably have had moments in which Mother Earth whispered to you, even if you were not consciously aware of the source: the beautiful sunset that helped you forget the day's tension, the robin whose song was a lofty angelic hymn, the unconditional love that a mother cat extended to her offspring that reminded you of God's love for you, the snail that you observed in your garden whose unruffled persistence in crossing the flower bed helped strengthen your own resolve on a difficult matter—*Mother Earth speaking.*

Choosing our reality

> As a man thinks, so he is, and as a man chooses, so is he and so is his nature.
>
> Ralph Waldo Emerson, Essay, "Spiritual Laws"

> We can choose what we wish to experience.
>
> Ernest Holmes, *The Science of Mind*

One of the greatest spiritual gifts that God, the Divine Creative Intelligence, has given us is the ability to create our own reality—our own experience of life—through the power of choice. When we *choose* (consciously or unconsciously) to focus our mind upon a particular thought, impression, or imaginative nuance, that thought or impression we have chosen will become our reality for the moment. Reality is a matter of choice.

Thomas Berry's book, *The Dream of the Earth,* illustrates the effect Mother Earth can have upon our ability to create our own reality. He writes:

> If we have powers of imagination, they are activated by the magic display of color and sound, of form and movement, such as we observe in the clouds of

the sky, the trees and bushes and flowers, the waters and the wind, the singing birds, and the movement of the great blue whale through the sea.

Mother Earth stimulates and nourishes our imagination. Her beauty and harmony show us what is possible for our own lives. We can *choose* to experience Mother Earth as a sacred and beautiful expression of God and allow her principles to inspire and to guide us in a life of beauty, harmony, and peace.

Exercising our choice—A sacred alliance

We must go out and re-ally ourselves with nature every day.

Henry Thoreau, *Walden*

Thoreau proposes a choice we can make regarding our relationship with Mother Earth. We can choose to establish an alliance—an intimate spiritual relationship—between ourselves and Mother Earth. Consider for a moment the following potential benefits of creating an intimate alliance with Mother Earth. Reflect upon the degree that you presently experience each benefit in your life. If you feel there are other benefits which may emanate from an alliance with Mother Earth, please add them to the list.

Potential Benefits of an
Alliance with Nature/Mother Earth

- Greater appreciation for Mother Earth as one with God, the Divine Creative Intelligence

- Enhanced sense of unity with Mother Earth and the Spiritual Principles that she embodies

- Feelings of harmony and balance as we conduct our activities similar to Mother Earth's harmony and balance as she conducts her activities

- Less reliance upon materialistic values as a means for determining our self–worth

- Openness to healing metaphors to help us restore balance between masculine and feminine dimensions of life: Native Americans emphasize the balanced relationship between Father Sky and Mother Earth as a guide for creating balance in their own lives

- Less tension and stress; greater satisfaction with life "just as it is" with diminished anxiety over how it "should be"

- Greater sense of purpose in life; a sense that everything we do is significant; everything affects the Whole

- Fewer feelings of isolation from others or from Nature

- Greater awareness of our role in maintaining Mother Earth's beauty and harmony

- *Other*: list your own ideas

Creating an Alliance with Mother Earth

An alliance requires several essential ingredients. Reflect upon the ideas below and how you can address them to create your personal alliance with Mother Earth. An alliance needs these elements:

- Recognition of the need to envision a new, more desirable relationship with Mother Earth than the one presently experienced

- An active, conscious desire to create the new, more desirable relationship

- Recognizing our Oneness with Mother Earth and with God

- An initial implementation period in which we must work diligently to create the alliance and long–term nurturing to sustain the alliance

- Patience even when our culture offers little support for—or may resist—our efforts to create an alliance with Mother Earth

- Awareness that the benefits of intimacy with Mother Earth will be greater than the mere sum of its parts—*Synergy*

Once you have explored the benefits of and ingredients for creating an alliance with Mother Earth, you will have established a foundation for your task. The steps that follow offer suggestions for your task. They incorporate activities for both the **head/mind** (thinking, reading, analyzing, etc.) and the **heart/intuition** (meditation, rituals, personal experience, etc.) portions of our psyche. We are both head/mind and heart/intuition beings. Using these resources empowers us for growth.

STEP ONE: CREATE YOUR VISION

Suggestions for the head/mind approach to envisioning

- Explore the beliefs and traditions of people who currently and historically have experienced intimacy with Mother Earth. You can find examples in many cultures. Use the ones that most appeal to you from this and other books.

- Read the poetry of Whitman, Wordsworth, May Sarton, Joy Harjo, Wendell Berry, Mary Oliver, Zen poets from China and Japan, and others to whom Mother Earth speaks. Make note of any insights that may emerge from your readings.

- Read essays and prose of Henry Thoreau, Annie Dillard, Myrtle Fillmore, Ralph Waldo Emerson, N. Scott Momaday, and others whose writings reveal Spirit in Nature.

- List ways these people and cultures envisioned themselves and envisioned Mother Earth.

- List the benefits for themselves and for Mother Earth of their spiritual alliance.

- Create a list of ideas and insights that you feel are essential to experiencing your own personal alliance with Mother Earth.

- Meditate upon the insights you generated during your explorations to send the vision to the deeper levels of your being. Envision what an intimate alliance with Mother Earth would mean and what you must do to create it.

- Use affirmations to deepen your awareness of Mother Earth's harmony and balance. The Mother Earth Sacred Calendar (beginning on page 142) has affirmations to use on Mother Earth sacred days and on other occasions.

Suggestions for the heart/intuition approach to envisioning

- Experience through rituals, ceremonies, or personal encounters an intimate alliance with Mother Earth (use the rituals in Part Four of this book and refer to the Mother Earth Resources in Part Five). Rituals that help us really with Mother Earth include the sacred acts of preparing and eating our foods and celebrating important Mother Earth Sacred Events such as the Solstices and Equinoxes.

• Allow Mother Earth to stimulate your imagination. Ernest Holmes, author of *The Science of Mind*, calls our imagination a Divine Gift that God has given us to use in creating our reality. Use this gift to create expressions—such as poetry or art—of your intimacy with Mother Earth (Note: the essays and poetry in Part Three of this book emerged from the authors' creative alliances with Mother Earth).

• Listen to Mother Earth with your spiritual ears: "What is needed on our part is the capacity for listening to what the earth is telling us."

Thomas Berry, *The Dream of the Earth*

• Experience your intimacy with Mother Earth at the deeper levels of your being during your meditations. Allow impressions and insights about living in a sacred alliance with Mother Earth to emerge spontaneously. Do not think about them—just allow them to "bubble up" on their own. Simply *be* one with her.

STEP TWO: LIVE YOUR VISION

Suggestions incorporating head/mind and heart/intuition activities

• Create affirmations that honor and emphasize your sacred alliance with Mother Earth (see the Mother Earth Sacred Calendar for examples).

- Develop and maintain mindful awareness of your actions and how they affect Mother Earth; pay attention to how you interact with Mother Earth as you conduct your daily affairs.

- Call upon your relationship whenever you must make a decision. Allow your relationship with her to be a guiding influence in making the decision. Remember, Mother Earth is a spiritual being whose basic nature emphasizes harmony and balance. She patiently awaits our willingness to receive her guidance. For ideas, refer to the Native American Rituals beginning on page 102.

- Spend "mindful" time with Mother Earth. Mindful time is when you relax and allow yourself and Mother Earth to become one for the moment. Mindful time is sacred time in which *being* is primary and *doing* is secondary. Your *doing* activities are grounded in *being* one with Mother Earth.

- Be aware of your alliance when your chores or recreational activities place you in Nature (gardening, hiking, or camping). Notice how you interact with Mother Earth as you conduct these activities. Eventually, your awareness may lead to being more intimate with Mother Earth while you perform the activities.

- Tithe your time, money, and energy to organizations, spiritual groups, projects, or activities that benefit Mother Earth (see pages 207 to 218 of the Resource Section for a list of groups and activities).

- Give thanks, both silently and aloud, whenever you become aware of ways in which you are living more harmoniously with Mother Earth.

- Continue to meditate.

STEP THREE: SHARE YOUR VISION

Suggestions incorporating head/mind and heart/intuition activities

- Recognize that each person is free to create his or her own reality and his or her personal relationship with Mother Earth. This freedom is God's gift to each of us. We must grant others the freedom to construct their own reality which will be different from ours, as each of us is unique. We do not respond very well to being told what we *should* do or how we *should* act. We respond more favorably to loving, nonjudgmental examples set by others.

- Recognize the futility and counterproductiveness of condemning or judging the behavior of others who may not experience the sacredness of Mother Earth. Condemning others only adds negative energy to life; it usually does not stimulate changes in behavior.

- Lovingly and nonjudgmentally share your insights with others and support their efforts to create an alliance with Mother Earth.

- Give thanks, both silently and aloud, whenever you observe another person living intimately with Mother Earth.

- Continue to meditate.

Creating an intimate spiritual relationship with Mother Earth and the Divinity she embodies will be a challenge; however, the Universal Creative Mind has given us sufficient resources for the task. We empower ourselves to use these resources when we put aside anger and resentment over the past and accept the responsibility for creating the future by using the gift of choice. *Choose wisely.*

> There must be new contact between men and the earth; the earth must be newly seen and heard and felt and smelled and tasted; there must be a renewal of the wisdom that comes with knowing clearly the pain and the pleasure and the risk and the responsibility of being alive.
>
> Wendell Berry, *A Continuous Harmony*

•   •   •

Notes: There has been considerable movement within mainstream Judaism and Christianity toward creating a sacred alliance with Mother Earth. "Eco–spiritual" organizations within several major denominations have emerged, as have eco–spiritual groups adjunct to other denominations. Readers may find organizations suited to their traditional spiritual orientation that seek ways to celebrate the sacredness of Mother Earth. For a list of these eco–spiritual organizations, please refer to pages 207 through 218 in the Resource Section.

Also, indigenous peoples of the world, as well as many Western mystics, emphasize balance between Mother Earth and Father Sky (i.e., between the feminine and masculine creative energies of the universe). For examples of this balanced relationship that each of us can experience, please refer to the myths in Part Two and to the Native American Rituals and Solstice Rituals in Part Four. Mother Earth and Father Sky—*partners.*

> All is beautiful, indeed.
> Now Mother Earth
> And Father Sky
> Meeting, joining one another,
> Helpmates always.
> All is beautiful, indeed.

Navajo Prayer for Mother Earth and Father Sky

Praised be You, my Lord, with all your creatures, especially Brother Sun, who is the day and through him You give us light.

Praised be You, my Lord, through our Sister Mother Earth, who sustains and governs us and produces varied fruits, flowers, and herbs.

St. Francis of Assisi,
excerpt from "Canticle of Brother Sun and Sister Moon"

— *John McMurphy*

— Suggested Readings —

Thomas Berry, *The Dream of the Earth*, Sierra Club Books

Wendell Berry, *A Continuous Harmony*, Harcourt, Brace, Jovanovich

Joseph Campbell, *The Mythic Image*, Princeton University Press

Michael J. Cohen, *Connecting with Nature*, University of Global Education (see page 218)

Mircea Eliade, *A History of Religious Ideas, Volumes 1 and 2*, University of Chicago Press

Myrtle Fillmore, *Letters of Myrtle Fillmore*, Unity Village

Matthew Fox, *The Coming of the Cosmic Christ*, Harper & Row

Matthew Fox (ed.), *Western Spirituality*, Bear & Company

Marija Gimbutas, *The Language of the Goddess*, Harper and Row

Ernest Holmes, *The Science of Mind*, Putnam's

Ursula King (ed.), *Women in the World's Religions*, Paragon House

Alexander Marshack, *The Roots of Civilization*, Moyer Bell

Elizabeth Cady Stanton, *The Woman's Bible*, Northeastern University Press

Alan Watts, *Myth and Ritual in Christianity,* Beacon Press

PART TWO
Mother Earth Mythologies

Every mythology is "true." Mythology is the wisdom of life as it relates to a specific culture at a specific time. It integrates people into their society and their society into Nature. It unites Nature with my nature. Mythology is a harmonizing force...Myths offer clues to the spiritual potential of human life.

Joseph Campbell, *The Power of Myth*

Carl Jung, the eminent psychologist whose work influenced Joseph Campbell, believed that we do not consciously *invent* myths—we *experience* them as products of our unconscious mind's desire to create harmony and balance in our lives. Myths, therefore, emerge from the depths of our being into our conscious awareness to nurture and to enrich our journey through life.

Mythological traditions from every part of the planet reveal humanity's experience of the unity between ourselves and Mother Earth. The experience of unity is not limited to a few cultures in distant times or lands; it is the collective human experience told and re-told countless times. The myths included in this selection illustrate our universal reverence for Mother Earth and how our respect for her natural ways can create balance and harmony in our lives.

Mythologies of Human Origins: The Earth is Our Mother

Mother Earth, her life am I
Mother Earth, her body is my body.

Navajo Song

The statement "The Earth is our Mother" and similar declarations expressing unity between ourselves and Mother Earth frequently appear in Native American, African, Asian, and Oceanic spiritual traditions. This awareness exists in all parts of the world, because deep within each of us is the wisdom that we, like Mother Earth, are the physical embodiment of God. Everything participates in this Divine Unity.

Reverence for Mother Earth as the sacred entity from whose body we are made and as the one who sustains us throughout life is universal. Even Judaism and Christianity which no longer openly acknowledge the unity between ourselves and Mother Earth illustrate the idea through their story of human origins. A brief survey of the world's myths of human origins reveals the link between ourselves and Mother Earth that humans everywhere experience.

Myths of human origins

Judeo–Christian — In Genesis, God took dust from the Earth and formed human beings. In Hebrew *adamah*, is the feminine form of *Adam* and means "earth" or "ground." Judeo–Christian burial also reveals our ties to Mother Earth with the words: "Earth to Earth, ashes to ashes, and dust to dust."

From Mother Earth's body we came, and to it we shall return.

Egyptian — *Khnoumou*, the Creator of the Gods, molded people out of Nile River clay (Mother Earth) on a potter's wheel.

Ancient Roman/Old Latin — The name for our species—*Homo sapiens*—and the term we use to describe ourselves—*human*—are related to the Old Latin terms *hemo*—"the earthly one"— and *humus*— "earth or soil." Very early in the consciousness of Western Civilization is the awareness of our unity with Mother Earth.

Roman/Classical Period — According to Ovid's *Metamorphosis*: "The Creator took the Earth and molded it into the shape of humans."

Babylonian — From texts dating about 1700 BCE, *Nintu*, the Goddess of the Earth, creates human beings out of clay (Mother Earth) and animates the new lifeform with her blood.

Another version of the Babylonian creation myth has *Bel* (ruler of the underworld) cut off his own head. The other deities created humans by mixing *Bel's* blood with dust from the Earth. Yet another version of Babylonian creation mythology has the Goddess *Innana's* blood mixed with Mother Earth to create humans. Each of these three different myths features Mother Earth as the substance from which we were created.

Hopi — Spider Woman mixes her own saliva with dust from Mother Earth to create all forms of life. Spider Woman took four colors from the Earth (red, yellow, black, and white) and created four men and four women by shaping the Earth and singing the Creation Song.

Lipan Apache — The Lipan Apache myth says that human beings were formed deep inside Mother Earth, inside her womb. We later crawled up to the Point of Emergence and out onto the surface. Emergence from Mother Earth's womb/body is a common theme in Native American mythology.

Assinibone/People of the American Great Plains — *Inktonmi* (the Chief Deity) created humans out of dirt from Mother Earth's body.

Alabama/Creek — The oral tradition of the Alabama people says that they sprang up out of Mother Earth's belly at a place between the Cahaba and Alabama Rivers.

Nootka of Canada — A Nootka prayer states: "The Earth is our Mother. From her is born our body, and to her will our body return upon death."

China — One ancient myth tells of *Nu Kua* the Great Ocean Woman who gave birth to life on earth as she created from the waters of her womb all the plants and animals.

Australia —One of the many Australian creation myths tells of *Imberombera*, the Great Mother who came up from the ocean. From her own body she made the land, plants, animals, and people.

Yoruba of West Africa — *Orisha–nla*, chief of the divinities, fashioned humans out of dust (Mother Earth) and breathed life into them.

In each of these human origin myths, the name of the deity responsible for creating human beings changes from culture to culture, as does the process each of these deities uses to create us. Whether we were created by the Judeo–Christian's God or by the Hopi's Spider Woman is not as significant as is humanity's collective recognition that there is a Transcendent creative force in the universe.

Whether we were spun on a potter's wheel or were molded into form also should not concern us. The process used in our creation is not as significant as is the substance from which we are created. In each of these myths, Mother Earth is the substance from which we and all other lifeforms were created, indicating a unity between ourselves and Mother Earth and between ourselves and all her inhabitants.

Traditional cultures continue to speak of the unity they experience between themselves and Mother Earth. The unity they experience guides them in their daily activities and creative endeavors. Likewise, many of Western culture's most creative people—our mystics, poets, artists, writers, and musicians—have opened themselves to this unity. Their stories, prayers, songs, and art testify to their experience. Even if we do not presently fully recognize or honor the unity between ourselves and Mother Earth, the potential for its awareness lies within us. It patiently waits for us to allow it to emerge.

Lipan Apache and Assinibone myths paraphrased from
Primal Myths by Barbara Sproul

Other Native American myths paraphrased from
Native American Legends compiled by George Lankford
– and –
The Mythology of North America by John Bierhorst

Yoruba myth from
West African Traditional Religion by Kofi Asare Opoku

Other mythology paraphrased from
The World of Myth by David Leeming

The Mythic Image by Joseph Campbell
– and –
The Bible

Hopi Mother and Child Symbol

The symbol represents the intimate, nurturing bonds between our own mothers and ourselves and the bonds between ourselves and Mother Earth.

African Myths of Mother Earth

When people sing, I dance. I enter Mother Earth.
I travel into her body to get healing powers.

Kau, a shaman of the Ju/Wasi Bush People in Botswana
Exhibition note Harvard's Peabody Museum of Anthropology

"All over Africa the Earth is regarded as a spirit" notes University of Ghana Professor of Religion Kofi Asare Opoku. Among the Akan people of Ghana in West Africa she is known as *Asase Yaa* and holds a special status in their society. She is not a Goddess—she does not divine or give prophesy— she is a spirit in a class by herself.

Unlike other deities of the Akan or other peoples throughout Africa, there are no priests or priestesses dedicated to serving her and no shrines for worshipping her, because she is omnipresent. She needs no intermediaries; everyone has direct access to her. On special days set aside in her honor, the people do not work the soil or even venture into the forests. She is resting from her life–creating processes and must not be disturbed.

In the planting season, the people must obtain her permission before working the soil by making offerings and praying to her. Farmers scatter prepared food at the four points of the compass, and they sprinkle blood of sacrificed fowl on her body. Once the offerings are made, the people ask permission from both her and from the ancestors (ancestral spirits are considered the real owners of land in West Africa) before tilling commences. The practice of asking Mother Earth's permission before digging into her body is found in cultures around the world (see the Native American Sacred Planting Ritual beginning on page 107).

Human death also requires a special ritual for *Asase Yaa*. When a grave needs to be dug, the people offer sacrifices and prayers to gain her permission. The Akan, like many other societies around the planet, believe that humans emerged from the womb of Mother Earth. Death is a return to her womb. Before digging the grave, they pour libation to gain her permission for digging a hole in her body so one of her children may be placed back into her womb.

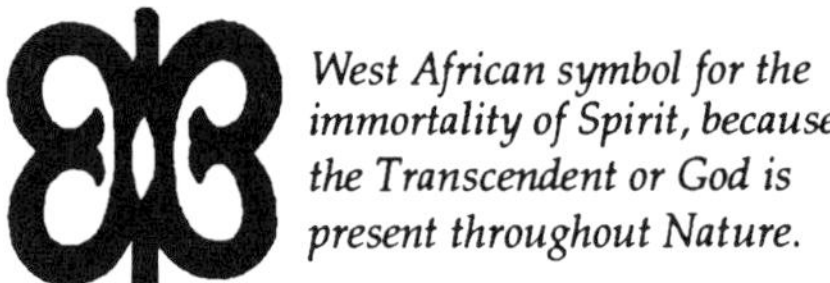

West African symbol for the immortality of Spirit, because the Transcendent or God is present throughout Nature.

Asase Yaa plays an important role in the moral fiber of the Akan. She detests those of her children who do not tell the truth. To prove the truth of a statement when challenged, people would touch the tip of their tongues with soil as proof of their statement. The community accepts the statement made in this manner as true. They know *Asase Yaa* would severely punish anyone who uses her body to proclaim truth when the statement is false.

The Akan's neighbors in Nigeria are the Ibo people. Here Mother Earth is known as *Ani*, the one who has given the Ibo all they have. The Ibo dedicate shrines to her and regularly worship her at these sacred sites.

Among the Ibo, *Ani* is the most loved deity and is the deity closest to the people. They thank her for her generosity throughout the year, but especially at the Yam Festival at harvest time. Yams, eggs, and other produce are offered to her, along with prayers and supplications for abundance during the months ahead.

Ani also oversees the morality of her children, just as she does among the Akan. She is the lawgiver for the Ibo and sets the rules for their behavior. The greatest offense anyone can make is to offend *Ani* herself. Crimes against *Ani* include suicide, killing another person, incest, stealing of yams or sheep, and killing of sacred animals. When someone commits such a crime, the entire community responds by making the perpetrator offer a cleansing sacrifice and by punishing him or her. Otherwise, *Ani* will punish not only the offender, but also the entire community by withholding her bounty.

Proverbs: Wisdom from Mother Earth

"Proverbs are the daughters of experience" says a proverb from Sierra Leone. Africans traditionally have an intimate spiritual relationship with Mother Earth, and their experience of her and her natural processes creates the wisdom found in their proverbs. Observing the ebb and flow of Mother Earth's energy throughout life translates into principles by which we can lead our lives.

Proverbs offer profound insights into human affairs and have meaning on many levels, some levels often requiring intuition and spiritual guidance to discern. As you explore the proverbs that follow, please do not rush to judgment. Allow the meaning to "bubble up" inside you however it may. Remember, proverbs are one way that Africans listen to Mother Earth's wisdom.

• If you want to talk to a Deity, talk to the wind.

• All that God created is good.

• Power is like holding an egg in the hand. Held too tightly, the egg breaks. Held too loosely, it drops.

• It is the heart that gives, the hands only let go.

Akan people of Ghana

• The moon moves slowly but it crosses the village.

Ashanti people

• When the moon is new, the stars brighten themselves.

Uganda

• Cactus is bitter only to those who taste it.

Ethiopia

• Love is like rice. Transplanted, yet still it grows.

Madagascar

Note: This chapter was inspired by my conversations with Kofi Asare Opoku during his visits to Dallas and by his book *West African Traditional Religions*. The book *African Proverbs* compiled by Charlotte and Wolf Leslau offers the wisdom of Mother Earth through her many African voices.

— John McMurphy

Mother Earth Mythology from Japan and China

In a leaf of a tree or a tender blade of grass,
the awe–inspiring Deity is present.

Shinto poem from Japan

Reverence for Nature in Japan has ancient origins. According to their earliest creation myths, Mother Earth was at first a shapeless mass existing within a primal void or cosmic womb. Then the god *Izanagi* and goddess *Izanami*—as equal partners—were given the job of stirring the formless mass with a long, jeweled spear. As they stirred, the mixture thickened until it dropped off the tip of the spear and hardened into a great island.

On the island the god and goddess were married and had many children. Their offspring included the eight major islands of Japan, many gods and goddesses, and finally the all–important Sun-Goddess *Amaterasu*. From her descended a series of emperors who were gods and after them the human emperors who were to establish a religion that would maintain reverence for Nature and her many spiritual forces. Shinto is that religion.

Shinto is as old as the Japanese people themselves. Shinto is a nondogmatic system of spiritual beliefs held by most Japanese about themselves and about Nature. Shinto means "the way of *kami*." While there is no precise English equivalent, *kami* refers to the Nature Spirits revered by followers of Shinto. The *kami* neither can be known nor explained, but they are believed to be the source of life. The *kami* reveal Truth to people and give them insights on how to live in accordance with it.

The *kami* include the spiritual forces embodied in natural objects and phenomena—wind, thunder, rain, rivers, mountains, trees—as well as the ancestral guardian spirits which protect and guide the Japanese people and their rulers. Chief among the *kami* is *Amaterasu*, the Sun Goddess who is matron deity of Japan and of the Royal Family. Her primary symbol is a mirror which represents both the sun and the *kami* within each person.

Shinto emphasizes a principle known as *makoto* which means "wholeness or roundness" and suggests that the religion applies everywhere and in everything we do. Most Japanese homes have a *kamidana* or altar at which the people daily worship the *kami*. Local shrines also are dedicated to the *kami*. Followers may visit the local shrines at any time, and many people go every day. Festivals bring people together at the local shrines for varying purposes. Some festivals celebrate an individual's rites of passage such as puberty, marriage, or death. Other rituals concern seeking guidance from the *kami* for one's daily affairs.

In addition to altars in homes and at local shrines, many major shrines have been built at important sites such as Mt. Fujiyama. Here, as well as at local shrines for those who do not wish to make the pilgrimage, people celebrate the three primary festivals: the Spring Festival which honors Mother Earth at planting time, the Autumn Festival which is a day of thanksgiving for Mother Earth's bounty, and the New Year Celebration.

Shinto is a religion of *makoto*—a wholeness that reflects Spirit throughout Mother Earth and our daily lives. Buddhism, the other major Japanese religion, also is a religion of wholeness. Since Shinto and Buddhism are nondogmatic and nonproselytizing religions, they co-exist peacefully within the Japanese psyche.

Mother Earth in Chinese Mythology

In China, *Kuan Yin* represents Mother Earth. *Kuan* is the Chinese word meaning Earth and *yin* is the receptive feminine energy which balances the active masculine energy of *yang*. *Kuan Yin* is among the most revered of Chinese deities and most likely evolved from the prehistoric myth of *Nu Kua*, the Great Ocean Woman who gave birth to all life on earth. The myth of life originating in the ocean contains truth. We now know that life did evolve in the ocean and later emerged onto land. The ocean truly is the womb for all life.

Water, as noted in the influential Taoist text the *Tao Te Ching*, is close to the *Tao*—the ineffable source of all in the universe. Water reminds us of our life in our mother's womb, as well as the ocean as womb. The water-womb metaphor plays an important role in *Kuan Yin* mythology. A widespread symbol used to worship *Kuan Yin* is the sacred vessel containing the Water of Life. The vessel and the water it contains represent the Cosmic Womb from which all life springs forth.

When Buddhism swept through China in the sixth century C.E., it replaced the worship of many ancient Chinese deities. *Kuan Yin's* influence did not diminish with the others; instead, it became an integral part of Buddhism which ultimately spread to Japan where she is known as *Kwannon*. She embodies the Buddhist principle of *karuna*—boundless compassion for all life. Today, Buddhists worldwide honor *Kuan Yin* as the Goddess of Compassion for Life on Mother Earth. April fifth is her holiday (see the Mother Earth Sacred Calendar).

Chinese reverence for Mother Earth also produced the ancient spiritual science known as *feng-shui* that is still practiced today. The Chinese have long known that subtle energy currents called *chi* run throughout Mother Earth's body, as well as through the human body. They also have known that these energy currents have significant influence on all life. *Feng-shui* is a way for humans to align themselves with these natural energies so that we live in accord with Nature.

For thousands of years, the Chinese have consulted *feng-shui* masters before building a house, temple, road, or bridge. The master discerns the *chi* energy patterns running through the prospective building site and gives insights to the builders regarding construction. This ensures that the energy patterns of humans who will use the building or road would flow harmoniously with those of Mother Earth. In modern times, *Feng-shui* masters contribute their Mother Earth wisdom to the building of skyscrapers and office buildings in Hong Kong, Seoul, Tokyo, Beijing, and other cities. *Feng-shui* even has found its way into the West, as builders in many North American and European cities now use this ancient wisdom.

— John McMurphy and Jeff Davis

Oceanic Myths of Mother Earth

Water all over, all over.
Darkness, all over, all over.
Aia living alive.
Aia creator of our earth.
Creator of our home.

Mekeo people of New Guinea

Papa–tu–a–nuku (also known as *Fakahotu* in Polynesia) is the Mother Earth Deity for the Maori of New Zealand. Her partner/mate is *Rangi*, the Sky Father, and these two primal beings lived perpetually "united" with each other. Together they parented the other deities such as *Tawhiri*, god of winds, and *Hina*, goddess of darkness and death. Their children, who lived in the small space between their two united bodies, became cramped and wanted more room.

Tane–mahuta, one of their children who was god of the forests, campaigned to separate the two primal beings of Sky and Earth. He said, "Let the Sky become distant, a stranger to us, but let the Earth remain close to be our nursing mother."

In Australia, one of the many creation myths tells of *Imberombera*, the Great Mother who came up from the ocean. From her own body she made the land, plants, animals, and people. The Great Mother whose voice is heard in the bull–roarer (a sound–making device that is swung on a cord in a circular pattern over one's head) is associated with the Great Rainbow Snake of the Dreamtime.

Aborigines consider the Great Rainbow Snake to be related to Mother Earth, because it swallows people during rites of passage and takes them to its womb just as Mother Earth does at our death. Later, the Great Rainbow Snake regurgitates those it has swallowed, symbolizing their re–birth from the rite of passage.

During initiation rites, the sound of the bull–roarer lets the initiates know the Great Rainbow Snake is coming for them. The Elders smear the initiates with blood symbolizing their death as children and their re–birth as adults. Having emerged from the Cosmic Womb of the Great Rainbow Snake, they now are members of adult society.

.　　.　　.

Note: The balance between Father Sky and Mother Earth found in Polynesian mythology is present in mythologies throughout the world. For Native American myths expressing this sacred balance, please see the Native American Rituals beginning on page 102.

Writing a Personal Myth

Joseph Campbell believed that myths provide clues to our spiritual potential, because they embody symbolic imagery from our inner, unconscious domain. "Imagery," according to *Higher Creativity* by Willis Harman and Howard Rheingold, "is the language of the unconscious, and the power of the unconscious is most directly evoked by the deliberate practice of imagery." Evoking symbolic imagery through myth creation enhances our spiritual potential and nurtures intimacy with Mother Earth.

Carl Jung often used mythic symbolism and imagery to stimulate people's self–realization activities. Jung, like Campbell, found a rich symbolic vocabulary in myths that promotes greater awareness of both our inner and outer worlds. Symbolic imagery, because it is the language of the unconscious, may not make sense to our ordinary conscious awareness. If we desire harmony in all aspects of our lives, we must make a concerted effort to link our conscious and unconscious domains. Myths are powerful allies in this process.

As we express symbolic imagery through writing a personal myth, we make it a vital part of our life experience. Writing a personal myth will help us access, explore, and understand our inner imagery by making it active on the outer, conscious level. The following items are suggestions for writing a personal myth:

1. Tell the myth with yourself as the primary character; however, use the third person (he or she) when "you" are talking.

2. Visualize yourself as the character you would like to be in your myth. Focus upon details such as your age; your position (wizard, princess, eco–crusader, healer, shaman, goddess, farmer, poet, etc.); your clothing; and your lifestyle. Let your character form in your mind, and make any adjustments you feel are necessary.

3. Once you have selected your own character, create other characters you feel should be in the myth. These characters could be representative of people you now know, or they could be entirely fictitious. Create their attributes as you did with your own character in step two.

4. Visualize the setting you would like to use. Imagine the countryside, the buildings, the time period, and any other elements of the chosen setting. Focus upon the sensory details of the setting (sights, sounds, smells, etc.) to enrich your mental imagery.

5. Allow the setting, other characters, and your own character to flow through your mind for a few days. Begin to think of actions they might take or what you would do in various situations. Search your mind for a possible theme that might develop. Let your mind explore the possibilities.

6. Think of symbols that you can create to accompany your story. For example, familiar symbols as flags, banners, spiritual icons, and coats of arms are a good starting place. Draw or otherwise create the symbols to enhance the

experience. Use the Mother Earth Sacred Symbols in the Resource Section of this book.

7. After completing the steps above, allow your myth to incubate in your unconscious mind for a few days. Then, when you feel the myth has incubated sufficiently, write your story. Begin the myth with a description of the setting. Make your description rich in sensory detail and incorporate the imagery and symbols you have created in the steps above. Next, describe your character, again using sensory-laden imagery.

8. Now you are ready for the myth to unfold. Write whatever comes to you, and try to refrain from being critical and judgmental. Allow your unconscious resources to guide the myth's creation. *Feel* the myth emerge from your inner world.

9. Use the personal myth creation process to create a play or dramatic performance for celebrating a Mother Earth holiday or a spiritual event. Native Americans, Africans, Celts, and others perform dramatic interpretations of their mythology to enhance their culture's experience of life.

Adapted from <u>Secrets from Great Minds</u>
by John H. McMurphy

PART THREE
Inspired by Mother Earth:
Essays and Poetry

Consider for a few moments the following ideas:

All who have achieved real excellence in any art possess one thing in common; that is to be one with Nature.

Basho, Japanese poet

You ask me where I get my ideas. They come amid the freedom of Nature, in the woods, on walks.

Beethoven

When I stand alone with the earth something within me going off in every direction to the infinity of the unknown means more to mean than anything...

Georgia O'Keeffe

What I know of the Holy Scriptures I learned in woods and fields. Trees and stones will teach you more than the words from the mouth of an instructor.

St. Bernard, Christian Mystic

It is the marriage of our soul with Nature that makes the intellect fruitful, that gives birth to the imagination.

Henry Thoreau

If we have powers of imagination, they are activated by the magic display of color and sound, of form and movement, such as we observe in the clouds of the sky, the trees and bushes and flowers, the waters and the wind, the singing birds, and the movement of the great blue whale through the sea.

Thomas Berry, *The Dream of the Earth*

.   .   .

Leaping from the journals, letters, and personal notebooks of humanity's artists, writers, musicians, and spiritual leaders is a reverberating chorus of gratitude to Mother Earth as inspiration for their creative endeavors. The comments above reflect the widespread awareness that Mother Earth not only nourishes our body—she also nourishes our soul and its creative energies. Intimacy with Mother Earth inspires us to express the fruits of our communion with her beauty and wisdom. Her innate creativeness nurtures our own.

Other examples of Mother Earth's inspiration

- Wordsworth and Coleridge took long saunters through the beautiful English Lake Country to stimulate their imagination.

- Richard Strauss took walks in the woods with his notebook and pen to record any music he heard flowing in and around him as Nature stimulated his imagination.

- Shelley was captivated by the light that danced on the water of lakes and ponds and found that this nurtured his imagination.

- Sir Isaac Newton gazed at the twinkling of stars until his mind became free of any distractions.

- Leonardo da Vinci became mesmerized by the shapes he saw when looking at clouds. He found that this enchantment with natural patterns and forms would stimulate his imagination.

- Zen poets in China and Japan frequently write poetry after meditating in a natural setting.

Even if you do not consider yourself an artist, writer, mystic, or poet, Mother Earth still can inspire a creative experience of life for each of us. Intimacy with Mother Earth promotes spontaneity, playfulness, acceptance of change, openness to new experiences, and a host of other attributes which enrich our experience of being alive.

Mother Earth's inspiration for this book

The poetry and essays we have selected for this book come from the authors' personal relationships with Mother Earth. As you explore the fruits of our intimacy with Mother Earth, remember that you, too, have the ability to experience intimate bonds between yourself and Mother Earth. Your experience may not lead to poetry or essays; however, it can lead you to a more joyful and fulfilling experience of life. We trust you will enjoy our creative efforts, and we thank Mother Earth for her creative nurturance.

Contents of this section

- Essays inspired by Mother Earth

- Poetry inspired by Mother Earth

Mother Earth and Our Journey

by John McMurphy

As you sit on the hillside, or lie prone under the trees of the forest, or sprawl on the shingly beach of a mountain stream, the great door, that does not look like a door, opens.

Stephen Graham, *The Gentle Art of Tramping*

Ralph Waldo Emerson observes in his book *Nature* that, "the happiest man is he who learns from Nature the lesson of worship." To Emerson, Nature is not a mere *thing* to be plundered callously to satisfy human needs. Instead, Nature is God in physical form. Nature, therefore, has many lessons to share with us in our journey through life. If we desire Emerson's perspective, then we must locate and enter "the great door that does not look like a door" to which Graham refers in the idea above. The doorway will appear once we create an intimate relationship with Mother Earth.

Ironically, those of us who "enjoy" Nature may experience significant frustration in establishing an intimate relationship with Nature. To see Mother Earth as a beautiful playground in which we can relax and get away from the noise, clutter, and stress of modern society is a common and seemingly harmless perception of Nature. Yet, it ensures that Nature will remain subordinate to human needs. Henry Thoreau summarizes how we may feel if this is our view of Nature: "How is it that man always feels like an interloper in Nature, as if he had intruded on the domains of bird and beast?"

Consider for a moment if you ever have felt as if you were intruding in Nature as you hiked, camped, sailed, or simply conducted your daily affairs. More than likely, each of us at times has felt ourselves estranged from the natural harmony and balance existing among other elements of Nature. As long as we believe that there is any difference *whatsoever* between the true essence of a human being and the true essence of other elements of Nature, even the most well–intentioned of us probably will feel ourselves to be interlopers in Nature. There is a resolution for this dilemma.

The universe is as inseparable from the universal mind as our ideas are from our own minds. When we fully know by insight the essence of the tiniest ant, we know the essence of the whole universe.

Paul Brunton, *The Wisdom of Overself*

Brunton reveals the prerequisite for finding our bearings within Nature and for avoiding the discomforting feeling that we are intruders. Nature is a physical expression of the Universal Mind or God. An amoebae, snail, or pine tree contains God's presence as fully and completely as the wisest or holiest human being. All are One within the Mind of God. Size, shape, speed, power, intelligence, and other attributes of the universe's physical reality cannot determine the worth of a single element of its spiritual reality. Once we understand that we and all other elements of Nature participate in a Divine Unity, then we are prepared to enter the great doorway into Nature as a friend, not as an intruder.

Mother Earth's Creative Spirit: Our Inheritance

by Jeff Davis

To say that Mother Earth beholds the origins of human creative inspiration may not be a particularly bold or novel statement. Many of us may be familiar with nineteenth–century sublime landscapes by Thomas Cole or nineteenth–century Nature verses by William Wordsworth. To more contemporary–minded readers, though, this claim of our creative origins may sound nostalgic if not archaic. Granted, for many of us, our daily experiences may involve computers and cellular phones more than magnolias and fields of daisies, or billboards and traffic jams more than majestic mountains and miles–away prairie horizons. Mother Earth's creative influence persists, however.

In her restless energy with what dwells within, in her surprising capacity to hold us in awe, in her shaping of bountiful life, Mother Earth gives us our human creativeness. It is our inheritance. Once we understand and accept Earth's capricious yet constant creativity, we also may become more receptive to our own creative impulses, be they in writing, drawing, cooking, loving, seeing, or being.

Dialogue

Between your lilies or rosemary during the spring's first hoeing, new stones may appear. Have you noticed, though, that the rocks' positions loosely form a ring? Each year, especially in New England, Mother Earth's belly turns and unfolds these previously hidden layers of rocks which emerge in circular patterns like craters on the moon. When Mother Earth's temperature shifts dramatically during the turning of the seasons, farmers in Connecticut, Vermont, and Massachusetts can count on contending with these newly "sprouted" rock patches. Physicists may refer to osmotic pressure in order to explain this process, but, whatever the explanation, this bringing forth of natural patterns suggests to me the essence of Mother Earth's subtle creative impulse.

One element of Mother Earth's creativity involves a dialogue between internal and external dimensions. Her unfolding of rocks from within reflects this dialogue. Just as rocks spring forth from the Earth's core, so too do words somehow manifest themselves from us. *Poesis* in Greek suggests a "bringing forth." This natural surging from within us may seem a common explanation for the human creative process: a form of "expression," a "getting out" of personal emotion. We may feel that something deep within churns and beckons to be released, to be brought to the surface. Yet, something more can happen in the creative process than solely a personal "inner action." An interaction, or possibly an interplay or a dialogue, can occur in which the inner realm—what English poet Gerald Manley Hopkins deemed *inscape*—converses with the outer realm.

The atmosphere alters Mother Earth's crust which in turn stirs her core and allows her viscera to fold in upon themselves and become part and parcel of a new top soil to be churned mindfully by our loving hands and hoes. Likewise, facets of the air, the soil, the polished oak desk, the plaster walls, a spouse, words written on postcards—all elements whose atoms constantly circulate and recirculate—mysteriously mix with the creative human being's inscape. Somehow, in an inexplicable mixture and surge, a word, a phrase, a sketch, an insight appears; soon other words or designs follow, and, perchance, they form some natural pattern. Ultimately the poem, the craft, the carving, the reflection, or the meal is turned over to others who, by virtue of their loving receptivity, carry on the creative process.

Perhaps in this dialogue we speak to the universe within and beyond what we usually understand as ourselves.

A part of initiating this dialogue requires that we pay more attention to what dwells within us: thoughts, images, sounds, dreams. Meditation, keeping journals, recording dreams, these are a few ways to get started. Another part of the dialogue, though, is to turn outward and to view the world— the diversity of life in our garden, the trees we pass on our drive to work, the animals who share our homes—with refreshed, intense eyes, ears, nose, and tendrils. It requires that we experience lovingly the physical phenomena of our life; Mother Earth is spiritual and physical, and her energy puts us in touch with the spiritual dimension of the physical matter which surrounds and composes us. "The greatest poverty," American poet Wallace Stevens reminds us, "is not to live in the physical world."

This dialogue finally requires being receptive to how physical phenomena affect us, impress us with images, and alter our psyche. This is a circular process which returns us to the first part of this dialogue. By listening to the peculiar rhythms stirring under the ground, by feeling wind whip through our crevices, by observing and meditating upon the patterns in an oak's bark, we awaken ourselves to a discourse with Mother Earth; for she, most naturally, impresses our minds and souls like wind's fingerprints on dunes.

By participating in this creative, transformative dialogue between inner and outer, between self and other, between experience and thought, between what is seen and what is hidden, between spirit and flesh, we reflect Mother Earth.

***

The Maker of this earth but patented a leaf....True, it is but excrementious in its character, and there is no end to the heaps of liver, lights, and bowels, as if the globe were turned wrong side outward; but this suggests at least that Nature has some bowels, and there again is mother of humanity. This is the frost coming out of the ground; this is Spring....The earth is not a mere fragment of dead history, stratum upon stratum like the leaves of a book, to be studied by geologists and antiquaries chiefly, but living poetry like the leaves of a tree, which precedes flower and fruit—not a fossil earth, but a living earth...

Henry Thoreau, Walden

***

Clouds—rolling, collecting, passing through space, above the freeway—portend to bring forth rain. In the anticipation, the waiting, the prediction, the surging, we hope what arrives and pours out is significant, fulfilling, and quenching.

***

Patterns of Earth, Mind, Life

Persistent attention to the dialogue between outer and inner worlds can awaken us to another dimension of Mother Earth's creative gift: a sense of a patterned life, rich and complex.

Thoreau sensed this gift and sought to give back. The way Mother Earth inspired and awakened Thoreau still influences us. In the *Walden* chapter "Spring," Thoreau recounts the phenomenon of the woods' and pond's melting and thawing after a severe winter. As he watches sand spurt from the Earth, Thoreau says he feels "affected as if in a peculiar sense I stood in the laboratory of the Artist who made the world and me—had come to where he was still at work, sporting on this bank, and with excess of energy strewing his fresh designs about." Thoreau continues to unearth a series of remarkable associations and relationships both between what he observes and what he writes:

You find thus in the very sands an anticipation of the vegetable leaf. No wonder that the earth expresses itself outwardly in leaves, it so labors with the idea inwardly. The atoms have already learned this law, and are pregnant by it. The overhanging leaf sees here its prototype. *Internally*, whether in the globe or animal body, it is a moist thick *lobe*, a word especially applicable to the liver and lungs and the *leaves* of fat (leib, *labor*, *lapsus*, to flow or slip downward, a lapsing; lobos, *globus*, lobe, globe; also lap, flap, and many other words); *externally* a dry thin leaf, even as the *f* and *v* are a pressed and dried *b*....The very globe continually transcends and translates itself, and becomes winged in its orbit. Even ice begins with delicate crystal leaves, as if it had flowed into moulds which the fronds of water–plants have impressed on the watery mirror. The whole tree itself is but one leaf, and rivers are still vaster leaves whose pulp is intervening earth, and towns and cities are the ova of insects in their axils.

Not only in the process of observing, I suspect, but later, in the creative process of rewriting and revising his notes, Thoreau again became receptive to Nature's energy. From perceiving how elements of nature pattern one another, he uncannily realizes the pattern of *everything*. At root—as Mother Earth reminds Thoreau who in turn reminds us—everything is interconnected and patterned: the root of a tree, the root of a word, or the root of our ancestry.

At root, our ancestry is Earth; we are "humans," from early Latin's *humus, soil, ground*. At root, Mother Earth *inspires* us; to "in–spire" is "to breathe life into" which is precisely what Mother Earth does for us, biologically and poetically speaking. But she also inspires us to create because of the way her marvelously patterned nature affects our psyche. Navajo blankets and Hopi baskets, for instance, beautifully exemplify their makers' "Mother Earth consciousness" in pattern and design.

By being receptive to the unified, multifoliate designs of nature, Thoreau's consciousness leapt creatively to the patterns of language, of buildings, and of the body. By being receptive, Thoreau's body mimicked the Earth's movements as the bowels of his consciousness and hands brought forth patterned words like the ring–shaped layers of rocks that likely surfaced in his bean fields. Such consciousness can influence the way we view and experience our lives.

Being Creative: Creative By Design

> My life is never ending
> For everything is a part of
> The roundness of the seasons.
> The sun is round—
> The moon is round—
> The world is round.
> And my life follows the same path.

from "The Roundness of Life," Ray Baldwin Louis, *Child of the Hogan*

But must we pack up our cars and head to Canadian forests or Arizona deserts or Louisiana lagoons for a few days to experience a leap in creative consciousness, to have a creative dialogue with Mother Earth? Not necessarily, although an occasional sitting mindfully in the garden wouldn't hurt.

***

Stop where you are. Grab a pen and some paper. Go to your garden if you wish, or stay indoors. For several minutes relax, close your eyes, and clear your mind of yesterday's difficulties or tomorrow's potential anxieties. Wait for several minutes until your mind seems generally free of images. Once your mind is calm and clear, open your eyes and notice all that is physically present in your immediate world—the top of light bulbs, the top of a coffee mug, your wedding band, the colors in an O'Keeffe print, a sparrow's head or eye, buds on bare tree limbs. Record and list everything you observe. Close your eyes and imagine more that is round—your baby's toes, Saturn and its rings, the Earth's journey through the solar system.

Record all that you envision. If you move more freely with images instead of words, then sketch what you observe and imagine. Play with connecting the two lists you have generated. Then imagine how these elements may reflect the circular nature of your renewed life. Record or sketch your impressions. Rearrange and play with ideas or images to compose a poem, song lyrics, vignettes, or a collage. Such associative consciousness is similar to what Gabrielle Rico calls "Design Mind" in her refreshing book

Writing the Natural Way. Attending to and arranging the shape of our lives is a creative and natural act.

***

A few physicists and science writers confirm Thoreau's as well as the Hopis' intuitions about the creative connection between Mother Earth and humanity. In their book *Turbulent Mirror*, John Briggs and David F. Peat note that several scientific discoveries stem from creative scientists' receptivity to "nuances having to do with certain 'themata,' that is, themes, that they perceive in nature." They also allude to James Lovelock's Gaia hypothesis to suggest that DNA's feedback systems for stability profoundly reflect the Earth's feedback systems for stability: a physical revelation of how Earth connects to body and mind. Patterns in nature reflect patterns in DNA which in turn reflect patterns in certain mathematical formulas which can in turn reflect certain musical patterns, as former *Scientific American* columnist Douglas Hofstadter—a remarkably receptive and creative mind—reminds us in his collection of essays *Metamagical Themas: Questing for the Essence of Mind and Pattern*.

What they're discovering, in part, is what the Hopi sensed hundreds of years ago when they told stories of their Creator Spider Woman: that we are intricately woven and patterned creatures; we are creatures of Mother Earth; by design, we in turn create richly, complexly patterned worlds.

By recognizing that we are, by nature, creative entities, we realize that creative inspiration does not necessarily require a trek to Chaco Canyon, New Mexico every time we feel our lives bland or mundane. If we understand that Mother Earth breathes and whispers into our creativity more through what we might call mind or spirit, we realize that, in part, we need only travel so far as expanded consciousness requires.

We can understand our lives as being full of complexly woven patterns, instead of monotonous habits. When we attend consciously to the small acts which commonly arise in our lives, for instance, we can awaken to a ritualistic daily consciousness. Cooking dinner, taking vegetable and fruit peels to the backyard compost heap, or taking a shower can become acts which align us with Mother Earth's providence and cleansing. Mother Earth's spirit does not dwell solely in canyons, caverns, and streams; her spirit dwells in the objects that have been shaped and brought into our worlds and homes; her spirit dwells in the interconnectedness of an automobile engine or a finely woven computer chip; her spirit dwells within our simplest acts and gestures which bring abundance, nurturing, and communion.

Regardless of our spiritual practices, we can recognize ourselves as inherently creative creatures whose consciousness reenacts elements of Mother Earth's spirit. Now, perhaps, it is time for we children to expend some creative energy in her name.

Of Dirt and Days Gone By

by Amy Martin

As a child, I knew nothing of concepts like the inter–connectedness of life. Conceptual thought was not my thing. Dirt was. Ideal for play was the sandy swath that served as a road next to my grandmother's house.

It was marvelously fine stuff, just enough clay to stick together. With a big old ice cream spoon swiped from her kitchen and a pail of water to forge proper molding mud, I would dig until whole miniature communities emerged.

It mattered not that a joyriding teenager in a pickup truck or an afternoon downpour could turn my masterpiece into a memory. The process was its own reward. I became one with the dirt, and we made beautiful things together.

My summer world expanded beyond my grandmother's small–town acre, beyond roads to places only a horse could go. There I found others who longed to merge with the Earth. In the slow–rolling, dry Texas plains, buffaloes of long ago would dig with massive hooves in ever–widening circles until craters arose higher than their horns, blocking the Sun, and the center pierced deep into the cool Earth.

I would slide down the slopes into the long–deserted buffalo wallow and nestle into the soft shady bosom of Mother Earth, peering upward into the blazing blue–white sky of summer as I imagined myself a Native American of long ago, racing on my horse with the buffalo to the brisk fishing streams further east.

One night years later on a Caribbean beach, I was blissfully six again–though nearly sixteen. Lacking even a spoon, with endless sand and sea water nearby, I scooped out great handfuls of beach until I was up to my elbows in an intricate wonderland of islands and rivers. Lost in childlike reverie, I was not thinking or analyzing, just being. Then music from above danced about my shoulders, ethereal strains too delicate to be heard. I looked to the sky.

A multitude of stars flowed and pulsated in a shimmering web until each one in the universe could be seen, turning the sky an argent glow that washed across the horizon to caress the sea. My sand castle seemed to melt and I along with it, as the music muted into the sound of light diffusing onto a forest floor. I felt the ceaseless flow of change, atoms in the sand vibrating in sync with my own atoms. All of it, atoms dancing. I breathed deeply, slipped into the dance, and knew that I belonged, infinitesimal–yet equal. And there I felt my soul, the soul of the universe, the unchanging essence of life.

A decade of torment ensued as I tried every rational and irrational way to recapture that moment, once again to disappear into a sublime feeling of peace and union. During my twenties, I chased the golden ring of fame and danced the tarantella of a lost and fevered soul, grasping at happiness that slipped away like sand against the waves.

Then one night in the darkness of a new Moon, I found myself standing in the mist of a huge fountain, weeping. Thousands of gallons of water a minute flowed down the sixty-foot walls, sheets of hypnotic waves falling into chattering chaos across steps at the base. Standing before it, my mind undone by the roar, I was drawn inside, into the thrust of the water, flowing as relentlessly, as seductively, as time through our mortality.

I had been searching for something that was lost, my childhood, the sense of wonder, the belief in magic, the humility before Nature, that was once so natural–the ability to trust and the ability to believe, things that became lost to me when I lost my childhood, things that are lost to most of us eventually, the elemental Earthbound truths of our existence.

Here, before this altar of rebirth, I began to lose myself within my soul. Transfixed before the illusion of water—yielding, yet all powerful—and the infinity of the sky above held intimate by the enveloping walls—here, under the renaissance of a new Moon was the magic, the wonder, the humility that had been lost. Tears of pain turned to those of joy, and I gently kneeled to touch the ground.

The Web of Recycling

by Amy Martin

An aluminum can, emptied of its fluid contents, is tossed into a recycling bin and taken away. Is this a profound act of community? A spiritual ritual? An ecological cure-all? Or just another version of garbage in and garbage out? Eclipsing the mundane mindframe usually associated with taking out the trash, a current passion for recycling has stirred people like no other everyday act, a passion which has more consequence than merely saving a bit of room at the local landfill.

The clattering of a plastic milk jug in a recycling bin rings with values we seem to long for as a nation, like the maturity of knowing that something out of sight is not necessarily out of mind. In a country that sometimes treats irresponsibility as a virtue, recycling an old mayonnaise jar is a small but responsible act, a way of acknowledging that our habits as consumers have repercussions far beyond the check-out counter. To recycle is to accept that your personal action—or lack of action—has a definite reaction sometimes half–way across the globe, sometimes in your own backyard.

Every time we divert a container or piece of paper from a trash can to a recycling bin, it prompts us to question the throwaway society we have become. It suggests that maybe, just maybe, if we stop tossing away all this garbage, we might not cast aside our pets and children, our downtowns and historic areas, our elderly and physically or mentally challenged, when they become difficult to manage. By taking an extra moment to affirm that your life can influence others, recycling becomes an act of exquisite consideration which embraces community. It is a way of confirming that we are all interconnected in this web of life, something people living close to Mother Earth have long known.

It is not hard to see intimations of reincarnation in recycling, immortality through a never-ending circle of existence. Though Western religions teach that life on Mother Earth is something we use once and then discard, a trip to the recycling bin asserts a more cyclic view, echoing metaphors of the natural world—the flow of seasons and the phases of the Moon—for which our psyches seem to ache. In this ontology, we are born and live and die and live again, just as in Nature, just like a recycled aluminum can. These spiritual chords run deep, and recycling deftly strikes them.

In small, subtle ways, these concepts filter into our consciousness each recycling pilgrimage we make. The toss of an item into the bin becomes a kinetic ritual of humanity and faith. Who knows? Maybe recycling will transform us into happier, more aware and considerate people. Perhaps it will lead us toward lives of patient contemplation in a society that increasingly values all life as one. It may be our way back home to balance life on Mother Earth with the civilized destiny for which humans strive.

Moonstruck

by Amy Martin

The night was dark. The cats slipped easily about the blackness in pursuit of phantom prey. As I moved back and forth between the house and garage, the air hung heavy with conspiracy. In quiet anticipation, the cats stilled to a whisper. Then I felt it over my left shoulder, slowly drawing closer. I stood transfixed as a silver light spilled over my neighbor's roof line to the east and watched my own shadow magically appear before me. Setting down my chores, I wandered through the backyard, smelling flowers in the lunar light and dancing with my shadow. They found me later, watching the rising Moon weave through the branches of an evergreen. I'd been Moonstruck.

There are times when the Moon calls to me. In the deep of the night, I'll wake to its shimmering glow slipping between the slats of the blinds, and watch the cats, handmaidens of the Moon, sit upright in the bed and stare out the window. And so I'll find myself Moonstruck again, my robe wrapped tightly against the chill of an overcast sky, mesmerized by the silver illumination filtering through the clouds. Against this argent glow, the twisted majesty of an oak tree in winter is framed, its branches an effortless design, art from the process of life. My lunacy sated once more, I go inside, slip some mugwort under my pillow, and fall asleep to dream of trees.

The Sun makes life possible here on Mother Earth, it warms us, causes the plants to grow and the air to stir. But we are ruled by the Moon, our emotional tides pulled in its wake along with the sea. The Moon holds our desires, capturing in its cool gray face our dreams and longings, seemingly out of reach. It evokes the impossible yearning we feel when we gaze across the ocean, look to the infinite sky, or fall in love. It whispers to us—*let go*.

In its turn of phases, the Moon marks the cycles of our lives. The year begins, for the Chinese at least, on the second new Moon after the Winter Solstice, the longest night when deep below Mother Earth's surface the seeds of life begin to stir. Passover is on the first full Moon past the Spring Equinox, as all Jewish holy days are lunar; Easter is the following Sunday. For the harvest Moon near the autumnal equinox, the Moon rises at the same time several nights in a row, and the light in the fields moves without pause from the warm gold of a fall sunset to the liquid glow of a full Moon on the horizon.

As the gibbous Moon wanes, it peels off a slice of itself each night until it is a faint shadow without stars suspended against the cosmos, the old Moon cradled in the new Moon's arms, visible only by the reflected light from Mother Earth. As a waxing Moon it rises with the Sun, lost in the brightness of an azure sky until it swells into Diana's crescent Moon. But whatever the phase, the Moon is always there, the tides still pull, its enigmatic presence reminding us that there is only change: birth, death, and rebirth.

The magic of the Moon goes beyond lunar rhythms, for it is timeless. We have been ensnared by the goddess of the Moon in all her forms: Hathor, Selene, Artemis, Diana. She holds her unfailing mirror to our souls for us to contemplate the beauty, and the terror, of the reflection that we see. Standing over the forever sleeping, forever young, poet Endymion, she mourns his soul's unlived dreams, urging us to yearn for more, to look to our reflection in the sky and ask, "Why?"

·   ·   ·

Note: During the last Ice Age about 30,000 years ago, the Moon's cycle which affects all life on Earth helped stimulate the origins of modern consciousness, according to Alexander Marshack, Director of Harvard's Peabody Museum of Anthropology. Marshack found our Ice Age ancestors recorded the lunar cycle on pieces of bone and stone. The lunar cycle was important in all aspects of our lives. It told us when was the best time for hunting and gathering certain animals and plants. It also was important spiritually, because its rhythmic cycle represented harmony and order in the cosmos, as well as women's menstrual rhythm.

Reverence for the Moon as Sister/Partner of Mother Earth progressed from the Ice Age into modern times. Europe is named for the Moon. *Europa* is the Greek word for Moon, reflecting ancient awareness in Mediterranean/European culture of the Moon's importance in our lives. Today, the lunar calendar still determines Jewish and Islamic religious holidays and sets the date for Easter in Christianity.

– see Alexander Marshack, *The Roots of Civilization*

Children of the Sun

by Amy Martin

You who are the source of all power, whose rays illuminate the entire Earth. Illuminate also my heart so that it may too do your work.

Gayatri, invocation to Satryi the Sun God,
from the Rig Veda

The glowing orange sphere of hydrogen and helium that rises each morning in the east has motivated humanity for ages. We are led by the Sun and chase our destinies as it sets into the western sky. Without the Sun, there would be no life on Mother Earth. It warms us, causes the plants to grow and the winds to stir. As the flora of Mother Earth store solar energy through photosynthesis, oxygen is produced as a by–product, without which animals cannot breathe.

The ancient *Gayatri* invocation still is used as a dawn ritual each day to invoke the energy of the Sun in a spiritual sense. Yet it is also a visceral reminder of our place in the universe. We live on a planet—small, finite, and fragile. It teeters in a precarious balance within the solar system, just far enough from its nucleus star—the Sun—that stellar heat does not boil all the oxygen away as on Venus, yet not so far away like Mars where bitter coldness precludes the life we know.

Our solar system spins at the edge of our galaxy, the Milky Way, not too close to the dense center of the spiral star mass; otherwise, planets would be consumed in the conflagration. The galaxy itself spins within the universe, infinite and mysterious, an unfathomable vacuum of space strewn with celestial matter and anti–matter. Mother Earth, as sacred as she may be to us, is but a trifling speck amidst the cold, dark immensity of space.

The only thing between us and the cold sterility of space is a thin shell of oxygen and gases we call atmosphere. Inside this gaseous casing, carbon dioxide is exhaled by animals who must inhale oxygen for life. That basic gas is provided by plants who need carbon dioxide to complete photo-synthesis. This delicate equilibrium is the mystical *prana* or "breath of life" on Mother Earth. Too much of either gas and *prana* will cease—and so will we. Scientists call it the "greenhouse effect," when an imbalance of trapped carbon dioxide causes the atmospheric temperature to rise creating havoc in oceans, forests, and ultimately, in cities.

The Sun that sustains us and helps Mother Earth create the delicate balance between oxygen and carbon dioxide in the air now impugns us. Why? *Petroleum.* Combusting this hydrocarbon energy source in all its forms—from the gas in a butane lighter to gasoline in car engines to fuel oil to nearly pure carbon coke—leaves in the atmosphere a variety of carbon compounds, chiefly carbon dioxide, or CO_2, a molecular blend of one carbon atom to two oxygens. Yet crude oil itself is the concentrated energy essence of the Sun, the remains of ancient flora and fauna left behind as evolution marched on, finally to be covered by layers of rock, soil, and dust until compressed deep within Mother Earth.

Yet in this dark scenario there is light, the light of the Sun which may save us from ourselves. Biomass is the energy of sunlight trapped in Mother Earth's organic material via photo-synthesis. Jungles have big biomass. So does pasta with marinara sauce. As our bodies transform Italian and other foods into caloric energy, so is the biomass energy of plants converted into a form we can use, primarily liquid biofuels—ethanol, or ethyl alcohol and methanol, or methyl alcohol—and biogas, which is mainly methane. All are easy to store, easy to ship, and ideal for our present energy infrastructure.

Unlike petroleum hydrocarbons, creating and combusting biofuels and biogas is environmentally benign. A closed-loop system as far as CO_2 goes, when biofuels are used for heat or energy, the global-warming CO_2 released is always equal to the CO_2 that was absorbed by the original plant mass. Biofuels burn cleaner, do not clog carburetors, and produce less nitrogen oxide (an irritant to plant and animal life) than petroleum products. Because they do not have to be refined from crude oil, the numerous hazardous wastes created by the refining process are avoided.

The future substitute for gasoline, the demand for which takes over half of every barrel of oil pumped from Mother Earth, is ethanol, a product of simple distillation just like beer. Gasahol, a blend of unleaded gasoline and ethanol found mainly in farm states, is used to raise octane without the addition of carcinogenic compounds, which replaced lead in gasoline. Methanol, which can be converted to diesel for trucks and aircraft fuel, is produced by anaerobically (i.e., without oxygen being present) digesting biomass, another benign process. Austria, Brazil, Italy, and New Zealand already have many ethanol and methanol cars.

Remember your grandparents' Model T? Ethanol produced by farm wastes and manure fueled the original Model T and most farm machinery in the 1920s. Prohibition at the time was a boon to biofuels by dumping grain unused for booze on the market, making it a cheap source for fuel. In an ironic twist, our current increasing popularity of sobriety and vegetarianism once again is creating a grain glut.

Over twenty–two million acres of potentially productive cropland are currently fallow. They are part of the "set-aside program" where farmers have made a financial agreement with the government not to grow certain crops to prevent a glut which would drive prices down. Corn, a key biomass fuel, is one of the largest "set–asides."

Just the twenty–two million acres in the set–aside program, a tiny fraction of all cultivable land in the U.S., planted in crops suitable for biofuels could replace all one hundred and twelve billion gallons of gasoline we consume annually. Biofuels, produced from the organic materials (garden wastes and food scraps) that make up almost a quarter of the municipal waste stream that is choking our landfills, could replace another large segment of the oil we siphon out of Mother Earth.

Researchers are developing plants such as hybrid poplar trees and perennial tall grasses which could eventually produce almost ten tons of biomass per acre with no soil erosion. These new hybrid plants will need no pesticides or herbicides and will require minimum fertilizer and water. One plant already available that performs similar miracles is hemp. Hemp, an annual herb better known as marijuana, produces ten times more biomass per acre than corn. It also has the added advantage of producing a superior fiber that ranges in quality from durable rope to delicate lace. The legalization of the plant could be an uproarious upset to the status quo. Just say *grow*?

Call me prosaic, deluded, or optimistic to the point of irrationality, for seeing a green new world oriented around Mother Earth's natural rhythms and the Sun. A switch to renewable and eco-friendly biomass fuels could dislodge the financial power base from the petroleum industry and give it back to agriculture, rejuvenating withered farm economies and turning them organic at that. Chemical–free fields of corn and hemp fueling a nation of almost pollutionless cars. Clean, quiet community power plants. All animals, all plants, all energy, all of life ultimately owes its existence to the Sun and its capacity to help Mother Earth produce life. We are children of their relationship. Let's celebrate that fact.

·   ·   ·

Note: Native Americans are among many indigenous people who celebrate the sacred relationship between Mother Earth whose body contains animal and plant life and Father Sky whose body contains the Sun and Moon. The prayers in the Native American Rituals section illustrate this sacred relationship.

Our Spiritual Landscape

By John McMurphy

Reflection after morning sunrise meditation
Banks of the Colorado River

Mother Earth patiently awaits sunrise. With only a subtle hint of the Sun's radiance, she appears dark and lifeless. There is insufficient light to discern any details of her beauty.

The Sun's brilliance gradually perforates the horizon. Fingers of dancing light gently massage Mother Earth as the Sun's sanguine glow animates her previously indiscernible details. Where moments earlier there had been only murky shadows and vague nuances of form, spectacular beauty and order now spring to life. The Sun reveals the magnificence that is ever–present, even though darkness obscures it from our eyes.

The sunrise's transformation of Mother Earth now whispers to me a Spiritual Principle important for our lives. Before we discover the Truth that lives within us and ways to apply it in our daily affairs, we see only dim, shadowy intimations of reality. What we think is reality is mere smoke and mirrors, illusions.

Then, as we look to the Truth within our inner landscape, we begin to cast light into the hinterlands of our soul. We discover the innate beauty that we possess as children of God, the Divine Unity in which all things participate.

God wishes us to know our true state of being, a state in which there are no hidden details nor lifeless features, a state in which we are fully illuminated and aglow with God's presence in our lives. Within the darkest and most remote frontiers of our inner landscape, each of us desires this illumination. We intuitively realize that the spark is there, even if we try to dismiss its callings to us.

Just as we can trust the Sun to transform the darkest and most lifeless landscape into spectacular beauty, we can trust God's presence within us to transform our inner landscape into a realm of celestial glow. *We are the light.*

.　　.　　.

I believe that God is within me just as the Sun is in the color and fragrance of a flower; the Light in my darkness, the Voice in my silence.

Helen Keller

The Second Star to the Right

by Amy Martin

When you wish upon a star, makes no difference who you are. Anything your heart desires will come to you.

"When You Wish Upon A Star" from *Pinocchio*

I have always yearned for the stars. Out in the flat Texas plains, where I spent a lot of time growing up, the night sky wrapped around you like a cosmic womb. There were infinite stars and infinite order, so much more than the constellations' simple connect–the–dot creatures. In the city, lights blur the stars which can make us feel cast apart in the darkness. Trapped under the city's artificial glow, I sometimes forget how the nighttime country sky shimmers like a celestial wave.

On the plains, the stars were my childhood companions. I just knew, with all those suns in the heavens, we couldn't be alone. Pinocchio and Peter Pan were out there, and with them all those intangible things, impossible dreams. Stars were conduits to a child's sense of God, a place where there was no confusion or pain. The sky held magic, a place where wishes really could come true —if we only believed.

Then a little knowledge reared its dangerous head. This big kid who thought he knew everything told me that those friendly stars were just the light that had left them millions of years ago. They could be cold hard rock by now. What we see when we look at the night sky is another time, he said, a time that has nothing to do with life here on Earth.

In the wake of the revelation, the stars no longer felt intimate to me; they turned infinitely remote. As years went on, the magic slipped away, as it always does when you think you know it all. During my teens, I became adrift in apathy, dis–illusioned by the the apparent senselessness of adult society that values "knowing" over magic and mystery. Then, my father gave me a large, full–color book on astronomy.

It was wonderful. Whatever the convoluted state of life on Mother Earth, science was full of miracles, and the universe was full of wonder. There were photographs made through huge telescopes, ethereal images of celestial lights. That second star in the sword of Orion, a constellation I'd watched for so many years, was more than a little diamond that twinkled in the sky. It was revealed to be a nebulae, in shades of amethyst and brilliant white, spinning forth into the infinite stuff of life. *I wish I may, I wish I might, go to that Neverland some night.*

The stars in the sky have gone from the naiveté of Disney, to the mocking face of time, to images of life endlessly recreating itself. Knowledge can hold its own kind of wonder, as magical as the stars and boundless as consciousness itself.

·   ·   ·

The second star to the right, shines with a light so rare. If it's Neverland you need, it's like believing you're there.

"Second Star to the Right" from Peter Pan

A Vigil of Weather

by Amy Martin

The ritual spans all seasons. At the coming of a storm we stand on our porches or in our doorways, enraptured by the sky. The weather still beckons to some instinct deep inside us. When darkness descends in daytime and the winds begin to squall, we are enticed out of our dens to pay homage to forces over which we have no control, forces toward which we must stand in awe. Secure under the eaves of our houses, never straying too far from the door, we watch the closest thing there is to the deities on Mount Olympus in celestial debate.

Gazing upward, we behold the turmoil of storm fronts clashing over our heads. The clouds, so intimately low, roil with conflict, churning masses of gray and white that blast wind into our faces— the invisible, intangible power of weather. Sunshine refracting through the clouds creates light without shadows, bathing us in a feeling of timeless unreality. A great quiet descends, the squirrels long since gone to their dens. We hear only the muffled conversations of neighbors nearby and the whining of apprehensive dogs.

But the cats are mesmerized like us, calmly perched on railings and chairs, watching the nascent downpour brew. During these incipient moments, songbirds deluge the hanging feeder in an avian feeding frenzy. More arrive and alight in the garden like crop pickers in the fields, pecking fallen seeds and berries from the vines.

In the distant sky, a small owl makes a rare appearance. Tumultuous winds hold it aloft, the owl drifts sedately through wisps of clouds. Tilting its wings, it swoops across the face of the storm in a series of elegant arcs, perhaps in search of prey, perhaps just having fun.

Humidity fills the air; everything shimmers in the diminishing light. A clash of lightning slices the reverie. Felines scamper for their houses, the vinyl flaps of cat doors slapping shut behind them. Hesitant and scattered, the rain commences, fat splattering drops that merge into cascading sheets of translucent blue. Our ritual complete, the human voyeurs acquiesce to the storm. We retreat to our homes trailed by resolute dogs. The sound of slamming doors reverberates in the air along with thunder.

Suddenly Springtime

by Amy Martin

Over–anticipated but never over–rated, the beginning of spring means something different to us all. In the upper midwest, spring arrives on a quiet afternoon when you're startled by the echoing noise of ducks overhead, returning home to the lakes. For the deep south, it is when the azaleas and rhododendrons bloom, white, pink, and lilac swaths across every hillside. To my Dallas household, it is the appearance of the first purple martin scout. He pokes his head into each of the twenty-four holes in the bird condo swaying in the wind on its tall pole. Inspection passed, he flies off to rejoin his flock in their northward migration, following their mosquito meals to warmer fields that include my backyard.

Southern winds return in the spring and bring a touch of balm from the Gulf of Mexico, relieving the winter mustiness hanging in the air. There are few golden weeks when the air is clear and clean, when you can breathe deeply because the pollen has not yet begun to fall from the trees. Frost-generating winds sweep down from the Rockies. They come whirling into Texas and clash with warm moist winds blowing up from the gulf. The ponderous gray overcast of winter gives way to rising turbulence of white cumulus clouds. Between the advances of the flirtatious storms, the Sun bursts through, and the air resonates with a clarity of purpose and an optimism born only in spring.

The time right after a spring storm is a Brigadoon–like moment: magic exists—but for only a short while. We all rush out to breathe in the negative ions that hang in the misty air. Maroon carpets of fallen redbud flowers spread beneath the boughs. Once the Sun re–emerges, I hurry to a magnolia tree nearby with its large waxy white blossoms. Their lotus–like cups shelter captured drops of rainwater. A breeze comes along to shake the blossoms, and their contents explode into sparkling cascades of liquid prisms.

Sunny interludes between deluges spur a riot of plant growth. Almost overnight shrubs burst into pastel colors, a frenzy of blossoms that drift in the winds one–by–one until the bushes regain their chameleon green. Tassels of pollen hang festively from the gnarled gray limbs of oak trees. The bois d'arc tree becomes dusted with a subtle covering of leaf buds, so translucent and fragile green that the sunlight passes right through them, making them glow. Each week, the leaves increase in size until we can no longer see the blue sky through the sturdy boughs of green.

The sunlight of springtime is an animal's earthly delight. Cats stretch out in the warm rays of the Sun and lay their soft bellies against the cool moist ground, reveling in the contrast of temperatures. Each morning they take over the east side of the house, occupying windowsills, front steps and squares of light upon the bed, changing position only when the Sun has moved and left them in shadow. In summer, it will be too hot to lie in the direct sunlight for long. Dogs attempt to stir to life and shake off their winter doldrums. But spring fever captures them and they sprawl out in sunny lawns, noses in the air, lazily taking in the local canine news on breezes drifting past.

On bright warm weekends, we join the parade of gardeners patrolling their awakening gardens. We survey the branches of crepe myrtle and roses, looking for some sign of life and mourn yet another oleander that bit the dust. Down on our knees, we poke fingers in the grass to see if there's any life left in the St. Augustine and gently remove the cool weather weeds that multiply overnight, taking the dandelion greens inside to make a nutritious salad. Invariably we find the first fire ant mounds of the season, the workers busy in their springtime ordeal of resurrecting flooded tunnels.

Spring brings a new brood to the bird feeder. Sojourners join the cardinals and wrens. Smart purple finches, their magenta heads glistening in the sunlight, lead the subtle mourning doves in passing through. All are comrades–in–beaks against the squirrel that is intent on raiding their sunflower seeds. Their territorial maneuvers culminate into a caterwaul of bird shrieks and squirrel retreat. In the peace that follows, the call–and–response mating song of a mockingbird echoes in the trees overhead. *Spring is here.*

Finally, the Fall

by Amy Martin

When the first hint of fall arrives in Texas, when we can draw a cool breath deep into our lungs at night, we tentatively emerge from our air–conditioned dens where we have ensconced ourselves since June to linger on the front stoop in conversation and lie beneath the trees whose limbs droop with pecans. Squirrels busily begin raiding the nuts, burying them in the yard where they will sprout next year. Shaking out of their summer stupor, dogs tug at the fence for a ramble through the park.

We slip into the leeward side of the seasons as the Autumnal Equinox arrives. Rain changes in the fall from the thrashing thunderstorms of summer to the enveloping downpour that comes with cold fronts from the north. The sky, once a pale sun–bleached blue, regains its deeper hue. Gardens come back to life, returning to their springtime emerald green from summer's parchment brown. Plants shed their leathery sunburned foliage and unfurl their leaves to soak the sun's fading rays as it rises lower in the autumn sky. Crimson spider lilies sway on long stalks, luring south–bound hummingbirds to visit for a nectar's drink. The brassy gold and auburn mums bloom to linger past the frost.

Fall beckons long afternoon drives in the country to watch tractors cutting vast fields of hay and farmers plowing the harvest's stubble to fallow until the spring. Breaking from our cars, the smell of bonfires in the air, we walk through the woods amidst falling leaves and tarry for the sunset. Golden rays cast their subtle warmth on lakes rimmed with the red and yellow oaks of autumn, adorned with bobbing flotillas of migrating fowl.

We eagerly pull sweaters smelling of cedar from drawers, grab our jackets from the back of the closet, and pull on thick socks. Pumpkins appear on front steps. Dew sparkles on the morning grass.

Mother Earth's fall holidays lie before us, a time for turning inward. We draw together as the days grow shorter, the nights get colder, and morning dew turns into frost. A fire burns in the fireplace, and in its flames we see the passion of ideas turning into the embers of desire that will fertilize seeds of change. Harvest in the fields awaits, the fruition of last year's vision ignited for a season in the Sun.

Mother Earth's Synergism

by John McMurphy

God manifests through everything...All is Divinity and Nature herself is the body of God. The mechanical laws of nature are set and immutable, but the spontaneous recognition of these laws gives us the power to bring them into practical use in everyday life and experience.

Ernest Holmes, *The Science of Mind*

Recent hurricanes, tornadoes, floods, volcanoes, and earthquakes have led many people to speak of the consequences of these natural events as "tragedies." The consequences of these events are real and do change the course of our lives; however, perceiving them as "tragic" distorts our perception of Mother Earth and the Spiritual Principles she embodies.

Perceiving the consequences of Mother Earth's natural processes as "tragic" seems to be the unique perspective of European Civilization; indigenous peoples of the world do not have this perspective. Since the days of Aristotle, whenever we call something a "tragedy," we imply that a fault or a flaw is responsible for some misfortune inflicted upon humanity. The flaw ultimately springs to life and causes the tragic consequence to emerge.

Mother Earth, because she is God in physical form, has no flaws. Her natural processes, even when they occasionally take life in the microcosm, ultimately work to sustain life in the macrocosm. Forest fires clear dense older growth so that new trees and grasses may emerge, thereby ensuring the survival of the forest and its myriad life forms.

Volcanoes release the tension inside Mother Earth produced by her hot core, a heat necessary for life on her surface. Volcanoes also furnish rich organic material to fields, forests, and waterways. Earthquakes, tornadoes, and hurricanes play similar roles in creating and sustaining life. These processes are Mother Earth's creative and life–sustaining methods that ensure the integrity of all her life as Henry Thoreau noted in his journals:

> Every part of nature teaches us that the passing away of one life is the making of room for another. The oak lies down to the ground, leaving within its rind a rich, virgin mould, which will impart a vigorous life to an infant forest.

The interrelationship among Mother Earth's various processes creates *synergy*, a Spiritual Principle that manifests throughout Nature. Synergy means that the various parts of a system work together for the benefit of the entire system— even when some parts of the system seem to cause discomfort or havoc. For example, when a virus invades the human body, the body's natural synergism responds by raising our temperature. We will have the temporary discomfort of a fever, but the elevated body temperature weakens or kills the virus. We return to health, thanks to synergism in operation.

The same principle holds true throughout Nature. Even Mother Earth's seemingly destructive forces such as earthquakes and hurricanes are a part of her synergism that eventually will benefit the whole system. Seeing Mother Earth's activities as "tragic" may prevent us from discerning her synergism and the other Spiritual Principles manifested throughout her processes.

These principles, as Ernest Holmes suggests in the opening quotation, could teach each of us invaluable lessons that would help us harmonize and balance our lives. The major stumbling block to our leading a more concordant life has been our preoccupation with solving "human" problems: disease, poverty, drugs, war, injustice, infidelity, and hostility. These are not our real problems. They are merely symptoms of our increasingly complex lifestyle in which we have divorced ourselves from Mother Earth and her wisdom. Our true problem is that we rarely draw upon Mother Earth's harmony and balance as a guide for our lives.

Once we discern Mother Earth's natural relationships and the Spiritual Principles responsible for these relationships, we can use this wisdom to create harmony and balance in our lives. We must not forget that we are part of Mother Earth, nor must we forget that our lives can operate as harmoniously as Mother Earth.

Applying Mother Earth's Synergism

Listed below are specific examples of Mother Earth's synergetic relationships and how we could use them to create balance and harmony in our lives. Whenever you feel the need for guidance with a decision you must make, select one of these natural relationships and look for ways you can apply it to your situation. Through time, you may discover other relationships that offer guidance for living in accord with Mother Earth's synergism.

Natural Principles as a Guide for Our Lives

NATURAL PRINCIPLE------PARTNERSHIP

• Examples from Nature •

1. Partnerships between diverse animal species

Zebras always lead the annual dry season migration from Africa's Serengeti Plain to the grassy Kenyan Highlands. Wildebeests follow the zebras, and gazelles follow the wildebeests. The order in which the animals migrate each year demonstrates a dynamic partnership among the different species.

Zebras eat only the coarsest and tallest grasses. Once they have eaten and have moved on toward the Highlands, their grazing will have exposed the shorter and more tender grasses that wildebeests prefer. Once the wildebeests have cleared out their favorite grasses and have moved on, the gazelles will have an easy time getting to most tender grasses nearest the ground that are suitable for their digestive system. Any change in the order of migration would threaten all three species. The dynamic partnership that these different species have formed ensures their survival in one of Mother Earth's most challenging environments.

2. Partnership between closely related species

Six species of vultures live on the Serengeti Plain. Although all six species quickly flock to the carcass of a dead animal, only one species at a time will feed from the carcass. The other vultures that are not feeding sit patiently until their turn arrives. They do not compete for food before their turn.

Each of these six species of vultures has differently sized and shaped beaks. The ones that eat first consume only that portion of the carcass for which their beak is best suited. This makes available different portions of the carcass for the next species with different beak shapes. This ensures the survival of the six different vulture species.

3. Partnerships between generations

Salmon swim up mountain streams to spawn. Near the end of their difficult journey, their digestive system shuts down to divert energy away from the body parts used in digesting food toward the muscles used in swimming. As the salmon are no longer digesting food, they begin to "digest" their own bodies to obtain the energy they need to reach the spawning grounds. They will die shortly after they have spawned the next generation.

After spawning, their exhausted bodies fall to the stream bed where they will die. Their decaying flesh feeds small animals and plants that will be the first food supply for the next generation. Generations that will never know each other have formed a dynamic partnership that transcends death.

• Significance to Us •

Many people in Western Civilization perceive life as a brutal struggle for survival. These people see different species—as well as members of the same species—pitted against each other in fierce competition for Mother Earth's resources. This perception is not accurate, because instead of brutal competition *against* each other, most animals and plants create dynamic partnerships *with* each other for mutual benefit. Mother Earth has many partnership models for us to observe and to use as a guide in our own lives. Partnership is the natural way of life.

NATURAL PRINCIPLE-------INTERCONNECTION

• Examples from Nature •

Each of Mother Earth's life forms is an individual life unit; however, each life unit has a relationship with and a value to the whole; all life is interconnected. Native Americans refer to the interrelationship as the Web of Life. Each strand of the web represents a lifeform. By itself, a strand is not very strong, but each strand is woven together with other strands to form a web which is much stronger. Interconnection is strength, life.

• Significance to Us •

We can experience ourselves as part of the Web of Life and feel the strength that interconnection provides. If we feel this strength, we may feel less threatened by life's challenges. We also can feel less isolated from each other and from Mother Earth knowing the Unity in which we participate.

NATURAL PRINCIPLE-------SYMBIOSIS

• Examples from Nature •

Lichen, a union of fungus and algae, is a prime example of symbiotic relationships. The fungus part of lichen provides the algae part with a place to live, and the algae part furnishes food for the fungus, which is a parasite and cannot provide its own food.

Another example of symbiosis is the relationship between the breathing requirements of animals and plants. Plants breathe carbon dioxide exhaled by animals and transform it into oxygen that animals breathe. The rain forests are symbiotic partners with the lungs of animals.

Sharks are part of another symbiotic relationship. Sharks allow certain small fish to scavenge their bellies to consume debris from the shark's feeding. The sharks do not attack their symbiotic partners, because they benefit from the cleaning process. The small fish are glad to clean up the shark's mess, because they have an ample supply of food.

• Significance to Us •

Humans can cooperate both with each other and with Mother Earth's other lifeforms to create "win–win" opportunities in all our activities. Symbiotic relationships are Spiritual Principles in operation.

NATURAL PRINCIPLE------SUSTAINABILITY

• Examples from Nature •

Most animals consume only the food necessary to sustain their own lives. They do not endanger their own or other lifeforms' future by over-consuming.

• Significance to Us •

Humans can learn that the future of all life on Mother Earth requires that we live wisely *now*. We must create and use sustainable technologies and live more simply *now*.

NATURAL PRINCIPLE-------FLEXIBILITY

• Examples from Nature •

Trees and other plants blow in the wind or bend downwards during a rainstorm to avoid damage. Likewise, most animals will abandon their customary or preferred food during times of scarcity and will eat whatever is plentiful.

• Significance to Us •

We can maintain flexibility in our encounters and avoid becoming set in our ways, especially as we age. Flexing our "mental muscles" is healthy, just as is flexing our physical muscles.

NATURAL PRINCIPLE-------RHYTHMS

• Examples from Nature •

Solstices, heartbeats, mating periods, moon cycles, menstrual cycles, monsoon seasons, planting and harvesting cycles, and tides are examples of Mother Earth's natural rhythms. People close to Mother Earth feel these rhythms as intimately as they feel their own heartbeat. They use these rhythms to create balance and harmony in their lives. Even if these natural rhythms temporarily disrupt our lives, they are part of Mother Earth's synergy and her sacredness.

• Significance to Us •

We can learn that our life has many ebbs and flows, just as does Mother Earth. We can learn to live in harmony with the natural rhythms around us: "To everything, there is a season... Turn, turn, turn."

Note: The ideas above are suggestions to help you get started in applying Mother Earth's spiritual wisdom to your needs. Spend mindful time in Nature discerning other principles that you can apply in your life. Mother Earth is a treasure–trove of spiritual wisdom waiting to help us live a balanced and harmonious life.

Also, use the Native American Rituals beginning on page 102, the African Proverbs on pages 28 and 29, and the activities in the Resource Section of this book to help you discern and apply Mother Earth's wisdom as a harmonizing force in your life.

Poetry
Inspired by
Intimacy
with
Mother Earth

Awakening
in a moment of peace
I give thanks
to the source of all peace

as I set forth
into the day
the birds sing
with new voices
and I listen
with new ears
and give thanks

nearby
the flower called Angel's Trumpet
blows
in the breeze
and I give thanks

my feet touch the grass
still wet with dew
and I give thanks
both to my mother earth
for sustaining my steps
and to the seas
cycling once again
to bring forth new life

the dewdrops
become jeweled
with the morning's sun–fire
and I give thanks

you can see forever
when the vision is clear
in this moment
each moment
I give thanks   — *Harriet Kofalk*

Long ago
the ancients say
this land was free
and we shared it all
with the mountains and the sea
the birds and the trees
we lived in peace
long ago
before those others came
and built fences
by cutting the trees
dug mines
by cutting the earth
removed her blood
the oil that lies within
formed long ago
like us
who lived in peace

the birds sang less
without the trees
the land became dry
without the birds
to plant the flowers
and we too became quiet
watching our mountains die
listening for the birds
that no longer flew—
but still we lived in peace

what sustained us
through all those years?
the nights of silence
and the songs of the frogs

for we know
as the ancients said
this land will again be free
and we will again share it all
with the mountains and the sea
the birds and the trees
for we still live in peace
and we wish you the same
for we all are one.

*— Harriet Kofalk —Inspired by the Bribri, Indigenous
peoples of Costa Rica from the book <u>Earth Prayers</u>*

Moment by moment
I fling myself through the universe
like a star
or thistledown
I sail the skies
forever
free to choose
where and when
the creation that I am
remembers the whole
of which I'm a part
and to return
to the knowing
that began with a fling
return to the silence
return to the present
moment

it is here that I know
here that I feel
here that I understand
this moment

is itself the creation
of all the moments
past
this moment itself
creates
all those to come
because it is
because I am
aware
this moment

— Harriet Kofalk

Inside
each snowflake
is the intimate
ultimate
design of the universe

inside
each snowflake
is the code
for its uniqueness
an essence
so small
it fills the universe

— Harriet Kofalk

Shadow of the raven
on the canyon wall
flying
where mere humans
are left to dream
pulling their shadows
behind them

— Harriet Kofalk

Priorities

First
I thank the Source
of all life
for this life's meaning
then I can begin

first
I create the space
in which to grow
into new dimensions
then I can move there

first
I envision the garden
full of rainbows
and scents of nectar
then I can plant them

first
I touch my heartstring
and feel its resonance
with the harmonics of all beings
then I can share love

first
I hear the bird sing
filling the garden
with melodies beyond my ears
then I can appreciate life's music

first
I taste the morning light
with which to create
food for my soul
then I can cook   *— Harriet Kofalk*

Angels

Spirits of the sky
present in every tree
reveal themselves
in diamond drops of dew
in frost on a winter's morn
or in a passing breeze
that comes and goes
and leaves its mark
in silence
do we know their presence
and then only
if quiet enough
to listen
and hear the twitter
of their giggles
as they watch
and wait
for us to learn to play

.   .   .

Angel's breath
the scent of a Peace rose
without time or space
present
to the aroma
of life
breathing itself
awake
to its own being

— Harriet Kofalk

It's like holding an egg
this feeling I have today
so fragile
yet so strong
protected in its natural space
bound to become
the fruit of seeds sown
long ago
potential
to create
anew
the world
at once remembered
and envisioned
this moment
this egg of life
I have
forever
but cannot hold
another instant
lest its time go by
and its power lost
so I cradle these thoughts
in the mind's arm
nurturing them
into new form

— Harriet Kofalk

. . . .

*Leave my parts to the birds of Blake Island, Washington**

I have found a place to reassemble,

fall apart, and reassemble.
It's not the mountains or trees that shake
my body apart. It's the birds who call.

A heron's squawk, cast above Blake Island,
squirms inside my esophagus, my intestine, or
     some organ
whose name, place, and function I forget.

Ravens' squelches rip the air
as they claim strands of my flesh
for a nest in a Douglas fir.

A bald eagle's silent glide steals my gut
and leaves the imprints of its talons
and wings where my tongue once was.

Birds of Blake Island leave me in pieces.

I want an old man who sits on a log along the beach
to gather my scattered parts from the sand
and toss them to the air

so the birds can scoop them up
and across these islands
drop my name in ashes.

*Blake Island is the purported birthplace of Chief Sealth, Seattle's
namesake. The island is named after the European-American
explorer who befriended Sealth and who influenced the city's
naming.

— *Jeff Davis*

Stories of Sealth-Washington Cedar

A single log of cedar shaved into
a wooden

ovum canoe slits the waves. Eight rowers
born unto

the Northwest Coast water push and
pull, push and

pull the oars whose labor links
the river

to their hands, their sweat, their spirit.
Rowers dream

and conceive the warm womb of their
livelihood

that sustains their rhythm, chasms
from their wake.

.   .   .

Cedar now lifts finely shaped, lawnless homes above
the water for people who stay put and buy aluminum
canoes for recreation, people who prefer to rest lifted
above the water where signs shout "No Wakes!"

Time's flow, though, somehow pushes, pulls,
and twists stories' bedrock boundaries.

.   .   .

Somewhere in those lawnless homes someone may dwell

who tries to feel Ocean and Moon
making love

underneath her bed, rocking her
soul awake.

Someone's dead myth becomes something
else's lover.   *— Jeff Davis*

fragments from Seattle islands

• *stone dam*
Unsettled bricks clink underneath,
flag posts in the wind.

Crabs scamper unseen
under port wall stones,

waves reciting the names of ancient
storytellers caress the stones,

and a boy gathering firewood stubs his toes
on the stones and croaks what waves whisper
as he damns God.

•• *stones*
Waves move across the sand
in the complex geometry of stones' colors
or faces of spirits attracted to tourists.

••• *mountains*
Buildings sprout from the form of mountains,
          vertical bridges,
                    ferryboats with wings,
                              groundless metaphors,
trying to carry us as if earth
          were a cloud,
                    an island
                              in the sky.
I don't have to mount Rainier
          or Space Needles
                    to see the sky
                              embrace my feet
and the space
          underneath the rocks
                    where Hermes and
                              hermit crabs sleep.

—Jeff Davis

Trying to Avoid Earth's Hysterectomy

Off paved roads in Texas Hill Country, weeds
    smother a dirt road—
stitches on earth's belly. I follow the scar's tracks
until it fades into a moist patch,
a field unowned, but filled with half-filled sacks,

punctured cans, and faded skeet chips

Somewhere in this field whose insides
    have been gutted,
a subtle pulse welcomes me, hesitant,
to its home. No fence juts
inside of Mother Nature's bush

where cattails brush over traffic's lips

I pick up a gray peel, maybe a grapeskin,
a reptile's discarded coat, or a dissolving condom—
as if to excuse indulgence. Unaware of its connection
to a universe of bubbles, small as a snake's grin,

I tear the minuscule world I pursue

Then, limbs of snakecotton, more delicate
than dragonfly wings, crumble in my palms.
But with winds' sudden wisps
the seeds disappear to breed with the air

and breathe life into wilted wombs

My scalpels—pen, a journal, binoculars—
fall from my palms as I rest my ear in dust
against her belly: a heartbeat
sending me toward her uterus.

— *Jeff Davis*

excerpt – Gathering Fragments of the Davis Mountains

1.
How long has it been
since I have been
with my footsteps?

2.
We think we stand atop mountains,
but we sit among thickets

3.
The mountains exhale
the low, lonely damp clouds
and reveal the way home

4.
So much care underground
unfelt by careless eyes

Trunks scar where severed
limbs clear the path

Stones have been thrown
from the road

Clouds have doused the woods,
and words have been carved on stones

You have brought me here
I have brought you here

5.
How do we know
when to leave things alone?

6.
This cave's crevices absorb the Jumano's last cry,
the Comanche's last song,
the wicked wind's and rain's fingerprints,
the laughter and truck treads passing miles away,

and broken pieces of painted glass
held together by a faded label
that reads
ELOB.

We move singularly from there to here
trying to possess the wind we blow in
and trying to see in the wisdom of wrinkles,
in the mountains' veins in vain,
above the horizon.

— *Jeff Davis*

— *Acknowledgments* —

Amy Martin's essay "Children of the Sun" appeared in *Garbage* magazine. Her essays "Moonstruck," "The Second Star to the Right," "Finally, the Fall," and "The Web of Recycling" were read on KERA, National Public Radio for Dallas–Fort Worth.

. . .

Harriet Kofalk's poetry is a regular feature in the eco–spiritual journal *Talking Leaves* and appeared in the book *Earth Prayers*.

. . .

Jeff Davis' poem "Gathering Fragments of the Davis Mountains" appeared in the literary journal *Concho River Review*. His poem "Trying to Avoid Earth's Hysterectomy" appeared in *Aileron: A Literary Journal*.

PART FOUR
Mother Earth Rituals

The making of ritual is a creative act fundamental in human life. It is also a divine gesture...Through ritual and ceremonies we make order out of chaos. In endless space, we create a fixed point to orient ourselves: a sacred space. To timelessness we impose rhythmic repetitions: the recurrent feast. And to untamed or unbound matter, we give a shape, a name, a meaning.

Gertrude Nelson, *To Dance with God*

One of Carl Jung's most profound conclusions drawn from many years helping people access their inner, unconscious resources for growth and from his numerous visits with indigenous people in the Americas, Africa, and Asia was that the human psyche has an innate need to experience the Transcendent or God as an integral part of Nature. Indeed, there is considerable evidence that belief in and relationship with some form of supernatural or Divine Presence in Nature has been with humanity since the dawn of our species.

This belief has been translated into various forms of worship celebration in which humanity actively participates with the Divine Presence in Nature. The function of these celebrations or rituals, according to Joseph Campbell's *The Power of Myth* is, "to give form to the human life; not in the way of a mere surface arrangement, but in depth."

Participating with each other and with the Transcendent presence in Nature through rituals takes us to the deepest levels of our being. Here, in the mysterious unconscious domain, according to Jung, we are all one; we also are one with the Transcendent in Nature. Rituals allow us to experience our lives and the universe around us as a mystery—something our conscious intellect can never fully comprehend—which can provoke reverence and awe, as well as great joy, in the deepest levels of our being.

·   ·   ·

Real power exists, not in the external form of a thing, but in its secret, inner form. To reach that hidden world is the purpose of a ritual, while to record that meeting is the purpose of the myth.

David Guss, *The Language of Birds*

Be not lax in celebrating. Be ablaze with enthuasism.

Hildegard of Bingen

Native American Rituals

All is beautiful, indeed.
Now Mother Earth
And Father Sky
Meeting, joining one another,
Helpmates always.
All is beautiful, indeed.

Navajo Prayer for Mother Earth and Father Sky

Native American Sunrise Ritual

When the eminent psychologist Carl Jung visited the Pueblo people of the American Southwest, he found them practicing an ancient ritual in which they prayed each morning to help the Sun rise in the Eastern sky and to help lift Mother Earth from darkness. Long after they had been informed by European scientific knowledge that the Sun only appears to rise in the sky because the earth rotates on its axis, they continued to perform their ritual. Jung was intrigued.

To the Pueblo and to other Native Americans, scientific explanations are no substitute for their intimate experience of Mother Earth. They feel themselves to be an integral part of Mother Earth's activities. They believe that their prayers actually help the Sun to rise each day.

The following ritual is based upon the Pueblo people's intimacy with the sunrise experience. The Hopi, Zuni, Pawnee, Navajo, and other Native Americans also have sunrise rituals, as do other indigenous people of the world.

1. If you wish to join in celebrating the Pueblo ritual, arise before dawn. Relax and clear your mind. Begin to pray to the Sun for its arrival. You may use the Native American prayers in the section below, find your own prayers or poems, or write ones you feel honor Nature at sunrise.

Hopi Sun Kachina

The Hopi and other Native Americans celebrate the Sun and its relationship with Mother Earth through dance, ritual, and sacred verse. They use the kachina as a symbol of spiritual energy in their rituals.

2. Open yourself to feel the Sun as the source for light on Mother Earth. Feel yourself connected with its energies and ask it to bless us again with its presence. As the first rays of dawn appear, feel them as if they were spiritual energy patterns flooding you and all that is around you. Give thanks to the Sun for making another appearance on Mother Earth and let joy bubble up from deep within your being.

3. As the Sun continues to rise and the sky becomes filled with its radiance, experience how trees, grasses, birds, horses, and other life forms around you celebrate the Sun's return. Listen to their awakening process. Feel yourself as a part of Mother Earth's celebration of the day's arrival.

4. When you have finished, prepare for your daily activities. Whenever possible throughout the day, reflect upon your experience with the sunrise ritual. Feel your participation in Nature's activities and give thanks for this awareness.

5. Imagine if you greeted the sunrise daily with such a mindful and joyful celebration. Even if you only perform the ritual on Mother Earth holidays, you will deepen your relationship with Nature.

Cherokee Tree Ritual

When you walk in the mountain stands of cedar, among the wise old elder trees, anything you want to know you can find there.

Saying of the Lummi People of Puget Sound

Many Native Americans have a sacred tree ritual in which they seek guidance from a particular tree or a group of trees. To them, a tree is a wise spiritual entity whose wisdom comes from several directions: it is long–lived and has experienced many things; it is sturdy; it is balanced because its branches reach into Father Sky and its roots reach into Mother Earth; it is strong–yet it is flexible;

Trees unite
Father Sky &
Mother Earth

and it provides resources for many plant and animal species. Trees, like other elements of Nature, have much wisdom to share with us.

Many Native Americans conduct a ceremonial ritual in which they ask the selected tree several questions. They open themselves to receive a reply to each question. After they receive insight, they thank the tree for its assistance and offer it some cornmeal or tobacco as a gesture of appreciation (the offering is called a giveaway).

The ritual that follows comes from the Cherokee People and was taught to me by a Woman Elder. It is a powerful way to experience intimacy with Mother Earth.

Preliminary Suggestions:

• Conduct the ceremony upon a Mother Earth sacred event (solstice, full moon, or equinox), on a special event in your life (birthday, change–in–life–circumstance, graduation), or whenever you feel the need to seek guidance.

• Select a tree for the ceremony either by letting it "call out" to you and lead you to it or by selecting it for its beauty, strength, and spiritual presence.

• Direct one question towards each of the four compass directions (N/S/E/W). To Native Americans, each of the four directions has a spiritual significance. To show appreciation for the tree's assistance with your needs, you will offer the tree a small amount of cornmeal or tobacco after receiving each answer. Reverently and lovingly place the offering at the tree's base. For example, when asking a question at the north position, place the offering near the north side of the tree's trunk.

• Ask the questions and wait patiently for a response. Your response may be an inner impression or sensation, an external image or symbol (a vision), an inner voice or intuition, or an external audible voice. The tree may speak through other things around you: a bird singing, a sudden gust of wind rustling its branches, or a butterfly. Be patient and be open to whatever sign, insight, or impression you receive. Remember, in opening ourselves to hear Mother Earth speaking, many of us will be learning an entirely new form of communication.

• Stand with your back gently resting against the tree as you move to each of the four directions of the compass. Before asking a question, relax for a moment and settle your mind. Let all thoughts of your own personal experience dissolve for the moment as you become one with the tree and with the moment. After asking each question, wait for a reply. Remember, you may see, feel, hear, or get an inner intuitive sensation of experiencing the tree directly.

The Questions:

1. Face SOUTH and ask the tree: "Who am I?"

2. Face NORTH and ask: "What is my purpose?"

3. Face WEST and ask: "Where did I come from?"

4. Face EAST and ask: "Where am I going?"

5. Go to the direction in which you received the most "powerful" or "stimulating" answer. Place your forehead against the tree. Give to the tree anything (a problem, a limiting thought, a fear, etc.) you wish to let go of at this time. Thank the tree for sharing its wisdom with you and for taking what you have left with it. Hug the tree and offer it more cornmeal or tobacco. You may

wish to stand back from the tree and spend a few minutes in humble appreciation for what the tree means both to you and to Nature. Thank Mother Earth for giving us trees as guides and teachers, and thank God as the unity of all things.

Sacred Planting Ritual

Brooke Medicine Eagle, a Wise Woman, teaches people who do not have Native American heritage ways they can experience the sacredness of Mother Earth. One of her teachings uses the act of planting as a guide. She helps people experience each step of the planting process as a sacred act. Each step is an opportunity to experience intimacy with Mother Earth.

When we prepare the soil for planting, we are working with Mother Earth's body; therefore, we must be mindful of our acts. Native Americans pray to Mother Earth before working the soil (just as they do in Africa and other parts of the world, see page 26). They ask her permission to dig into her body and to move her about. Once they receive her permission, they thank her for allowing them to cut into her body. Then they begin to work the soil mindfully and lovingly. We can use their wisdom as a guide whenever we prepare the soil for planting.

Likewise, when we place seeds or seedlings in her body, we should ask her permission. We can give thanks to her for receiving what we have planted and for supplying the energy the plants will need to grow. We also can end the planting process with a celebration, just as many Native Americans do. We can offer prayers, songs, or poems to her. We can decorate her body or make an altar near where we have just planted using natural objects such as shells, stones, crystals, pine cones, or other objects to honor her creativeness.

Planting, then, can become a sacred act in which we experience our unity with Mother Earth and all her life forms. A special relationship will develop between ourselves and what we have planted. As the plants grow and mature using the energy from Mother Earth, we become co-creators with her and with God.

1. Use the planting ritual upon a special occasion, a sacred Mother Earth event, or whenever you plant in your garden.

2. Gather everything you will need before proceeding: prayers or sacred verse, objects to create an altar, garden tools, compost, mulch, and the items you will plant.

3. Clear your mind of any thoughts other than what you are about to do. Meditate upon the unity of all life and upon Mother Earth's body as home to all life. Open yourself to the sacredness of the moment.

4. Once you have centered yourself in the sacred moment, ask Mother Earth's permission to dig into her body. Allow her response to appear however it may: an inner sensing or impression, an audible voice, a breeze moving about the garden, a bird landing nearby. When we open ourselves to be one with Mother Earth, she can

speak to us in many ways—and we will *know* that she is speaking to us.

If you feel you do not "receive" her permission, consider if you have adequately cleared your mind of potential distractions. Also, consider if anything you are planning to use in the planting process might harm her. For example, chemical fertilizers harm earthworms and other of her natural life–sustaining processes. Use organic fertilization methods such as compost to work in harmony with her. She lovingly gives us her permission when we are open to receiving it and when we are willing to work in harmony with her natural processes.

5. Having obtained her permission, work with her body with reverence for its life. Reach down and take a handful of soil. It is alive. Use your eyes to *see* its life—earthworms, decaying plant and animal matter, threadlike roots, or seeds. Now *feel* its life. Feel the presence of life in the palm of your hand.

6. Once you have opened yourself to the life with which you will be working, become mindful of your acts. Pay full attention to each act of digging, spading, or turning the soil. Feel your energy working in harmony with Mother Earth's. Stay centered in the sacred moment.

7. When you are ready to plant seeds or seedlings, again ask Mother Earth's permission. Ask her to receive what you are planting and to nurture them as her children. Allow her to respond.

8. When you have finished planting, it is time for thanksgiving and celebrating. Thank Mother Earth for allowing you to work with her body. Use prayers and sacred verse from Native Americans, from other sections of this book, or from other sources. You may want to create your own prayers and sacred verse.

9. Use natural objects to create a small altar or arrangement near where you have just planted.

Suggestion: On the morning of the Harmonic Convergence in 1987, I collected shells along the Texas Gulf Coast beach where my friend and co–author Jeff Davis and I had camped to welcome the sunrise on this cosmic day. I have blessed the shells with prayers and use them throughout my garden. I also add items collected from my travels such as stones, crystals, pine cones, twigs, and feathers. In some areas of the garden, they are arranged as patterns or as an altar. In other areas, they take the natural pattern created by the garden itself. These items, and the use of them, have special significance to me. Find and use items that hold significance to you.

10. As the plants grow and you need to weed or cultivate around them, remember to ask permission from Mother Earth and to give thanks. Likewise, if you harvest fruits, vegetables, flowers, or herbs from the plants, remember to give thanks for these contributions to your life.

Native American Ceremonies and Powwows

Native Americans throughout North America regularly gather to dance, to tell stories, and to perform ceremonies that celebrate their reverence for Mother Earth and her ways of harmony and balance. The listings that follow are a sample of the numerous gatherings that Native Americans hold in every part of the United States and Canada.

I usually attend ceremonies when I am in the area, and a few of these listings are several years old. While I have attempted to verify the dates and locations for each event, I have not been able to do so in every case. Check for exact dates, times, and locations in local newspapers near the dates listed for the events. You may be able to get information from the various Native American reservations or tribal centers in the U.S. and Canada.

Holistic learning centers such as Full Circle and Rune Hill also offer opportunities to experience Native American ceremonies (see Mother Earth Organizations beginning on page 207). The Bear Tribe in Spokane performs rituals in many areas, and Friends of Creation Spirituality includes Native American ceremonies in their offerings. Wherever you live or travel, you will find ample opportunities to experience Native American ceremonies and gatherings.

When you attend a Native American ceremony, please keep in mind these considerations:

- Native American ceremonies cannot be analyzed by using rational or logical mental processes— they are *experienced*. In ceremonies and dances, the dance area becomes a sacred space. It no longer is limited by the finite dimensions of space–time reality. Open yourself to the infinite moment in which you can *feel* your connection with Mother Earth through these ceremonies.

- Most performances are open to the public. Always ensure that a ceremony is open to visitors.

- Remember, these ceremonies reflect Native Americans' spiritual beliefs. Please maintain reverence for their customs.

- **JAN: 3rd weekend**   **Texas**

Texas Indian Heritage Association Powwow
San Antonio

- **FEB: 2nd weekend**   **Michigan**

Honoring Our Ancestors Powwow
Marquette

- **FEB: 2nd weekend**   **Florida**

Seminole Tribal Gathering
Hollywood Reservation in Hollywood

- **MAR: 1st weekend**   **Ohio**

Miami Valley Gathering in Dayton

- **MAR: 4th weekend**   **Minnesota**

Heart of the Earth Powwow in Minneapolis

- **APR: 2nd week**   **Washington**

Northwest Indian Youth Powwow in Seattle

- **APR: 3rd week**   **New Mexico**

Gathering of the Nations Powwow
University of New Mexico in Albuquerque

- **APR: 3rd week**   **California**

    Keeper of the Earth Powwow
    Fullerton

- **MAY: 1st weekend**   **Pennsylvania**

    Corn Planting Ceremony
    Lenni Lenape Historical Society
    Allentown

- **MAY: 3rd weekend**   **Georgia**

    Chehaw Peoples Festival
    Albany

- **JUN: 1st weekend**   **Texas**

    Alabama Coushatta Powwow
    near Livingston/Big Thicket National Forest

- **JUN: 2nd weekend**   **Delaware**
    New Jersey

    Lenni Lenape Powwow
    15 miles from Wilmington DE in Salem NJ

- **JUN: 3rd weekend**   **Oklahoma**

    Creek Nation Powwow
    Okmulgee

- **JUL: 3rd weekend**   **Wisconsin**

    Honor Mother Earth Powwow
    Hayward

- **JUL: 3rd weekend**   **Ontario, Canada**

    Mississauga Powwow
    Mississauga

- **AUG: 1st weekend**   **B. C., Canada**

    Native Peoples Festival and Powwow
    Victoria

- **AUG: 4th week**   **Ontario, Canada**

  International Native People Powwow
  Canadian National Exposition in Toronto

- **SEP: 1st week**   **New York**

  Iroquois Festival
  Cobleskill (Albany area)

- **SEP: 3rd weekend**   **Oklahoma**

  Choctaw Peoples Powwow
  Canadian (Muskogee area)

- **OCT: 1st weekend**   **North Carolina**

  Cumberland Powwow
  Fayetteville

- **OCT: 2nd weekend**   **Alberta, Canada**

  First Nations Cultural Festival in Calgary

- **OCT: 3rd weekend**   **Arizona**

  Apache Powwow in Globe

- **NOV: 3rd weekend**   **Louisiana**

  Twin Eagle Powwow
  Shreveport/Minden area

- **DEC: 2nd weekend**   **Illinois**

  American Indian Center of Chicago Powwow

Native American Chants, Prayers, & Songs

A prayer is just a way of becoming really
conscious, really tuning in to all the
relationships of everything in existence.

Sun Bear, *The Bear Tribe's Self-reliance Book*

Preliminary Suggestions

1. Native Americans use chants, prayers, and songs to ally themselves with the powerful spiritual energies around them. As such, we must maintain reverence for their beliefs as we read their sacred words. Before reading the following prayers and chants, please clear your mind of any distracting thoughts through meditation. Once you have centered yourself in the sacred and peaceful moment, then open yourself to the energy they contain.

2. You may read Native American prayers as part of your daily inspirational readings. Their natural beauty and simple wisdom (like the African proverbs on pages 28 and 29) can be a significant source of insight for us. Read only a few selections at a time and record your insights. Periodically re-read various selections to give you more perspective. Integrate your insights into your daily activities.

Always give thanks to the spiritual energies around you when you receive an insight or when you experience intimacy with Mother Earth. To Native Americans, giving thanks for whatever we receive in life is important to living harmoniously with Mother Earth and her spiritual energies.

3. You also may use these chants and prayers as a source of inspiration while you perform other activities to re–ally yourself with Nature. For example, before taking a walk, read a few prayers to prepare your mind. As you perform the activity, pay attention to Mother Earth and to your intimacy with her. After completing the activity, record any insights that may have arisen.

4. You may use a particular chant, prayer, or song in the purpose for which it was created. For example, the Sunrise Prayers that follow could be used to experience the beauty and sacredness of dawn.

5. Go beyond the brief introduction to Native American Mother Earth Wisdom that we present in this book. Do what we the authors have done: attend workshops conducted by Native Americans that are designed to deepen our intimacy with Mother Earth. Native Americans' spiritual awareness cannot be put into a book; it can only be experienced.

Lakota: Sunrise Greeting

Here I am. Behold me.
I am the Sun. Behold me.

Hopi: Sunrise Greeting

The day has risen,
Go I to behold the dawn.
The yellow rising!
It has become light.

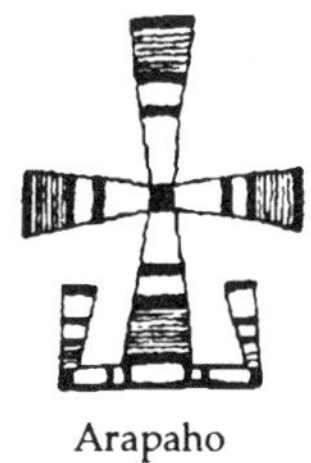

Arapaho
Sun Symbol

Pawnee: Sunrise Greeting

Earth, our Mother, breathe and awaken,
Leaves are stirring, all things moving,
New day coming, life renewing,
See the mysterious new morning,
Something marvelous and sacred,
Though it happens every day.

Papago: Sunrise Greeting

Come! Stand up!
Just over there the dawn is coming.
Now I hear its soft laughter.

Oglala Sioux: Sunrise Prayer–Inipi Purification Rite

O Morning Star, here at the place where the Sun comes up; O You who have the wisdom which we seek, that our generations to come will have Light as they walk the sacred path. You lead the dawn as it walks forth, and also the day which follows with its Light which is knowledge; this You do for us and all the people of the earth, that they may see clearly in walking the wakan path; that they may know all that is holy, and that they may increase in a sacred manner.

Kagaba: Song of Mother Earth

The mother of our songs, the mother of all our
  seed who bore us in the beginning of things.
To our mother alone do we belong.

Oglala Sioux: Prayer for Mother Earth

O Mother Earth, you are the earthly source of all
  existence.
The fruits which you bear are the source of life
  for the Earth peoples.
You are always watching over your fruits as
  does a mother.
May the steps we take in life upon you be sacred.

Iroquois: Prayer of Thanksgiving

We return thanks to our mother, the Earth, which sustains us. We return thanks to the rivers and streams, which supply us with water.

We return thanks to the herbs, which furnish medicine. We return thanks to the corn, and to her sisters, the beans and squash, which give us life. We return thanks to the Sun which looks upon the earth with a beneficent eye. Lastly, we return thanks to the Great Spirit, in whom is embodied all goodness.

Navajo: Walking Meditation

With beauty before me, may I walk
With beauty behind me, may I walk
With beauty above me, may I walk
With beauty below me, may I walk
With beauty all around me, may I walk
Wandering on a trail of beauty, lively I walk.

Pawnee: Hako Ceremony Song

We see on Mother Earth the running streams;
We see the promise of her fruitfulness.
Truly, her power she gives us.
Our thanks to Mother Earth!

Navajo: Song for Mother Earth

Mother Earth, her life am I
Mother Earth, her body is my body
Mother Earth, her thoughts are my thoughts.

Maya: Prayer Before Working the Soil

O my Mother, be patient with me. I am now about to do as has always been done. Now I make you an offering, that you may be forewarned: I am about to stir your heart. I pray you will have the strength to endure it. I am going to work you in order that I may live. With all my heart I am going to work you with love.

Lenape (Delaware): New Year Big House Prayer

We thank our Mother, the Earth,
whom we claim as mother,
because the Earth carries us
and everything we need.

Nootka: Song for Mother Earth

The Earth is our Mother
From her is born our body,
and to her body will
our body return upon death.

Navajo: Corn Prayer

My great corn plants. Among them I walk. I
speak to them. They hold out their hands to me.

*Navajo Corn Symbols: Most Native
Americans consider corn to be sacred.
Each kernel represents one person, and
the kernels united on the cob represent
humanity. Talking with the corn was
like talking with family and friends.*

Okanogan: Creation Myth

The Earth, our Mother, is alive. The soil is her
flesh, the rocks are her bones, the wind is her
breath, and the grasses are her hair. We live on
her body. All living beings—those in the oceans
and rivers, those in the forests, and those that
fly—came from the Earth, our Mother. When
we look around, we see our Mother everywhere.

– John McMurphy

*Sunrise and Tree Rituals adapted from
Living Deliberately by John McMurphy*

Eating as a Sacred Ritual

Food reveals our connection with the Earth. Each bite contains the life of the Sun and the Earth. Contemplating our food for a few seconds before eating can bring us much happiness.

Thich Nhat Hanh, *Present Moment, Wonderful Moment*

In traditional cultures around the world, eating is not the mere ingesting of food to fill our bellies. Eating is a sacred act that unites people with Mother Earth as source of our food and with God as the ultimate source of all things. Eating is a spiritual and a physical act.

For most people in the fast–paced modern world, however, eating has become just another of the many chores we must squeeze into our busy schedules. Eating–on–the–run has become so necessary to our modern lifestyle that fast–food restaurants now prepare almost as many meals per capita as we prepare in the home. Even home–prepared meals must conform to our crowded agendas as we depend upon pre–processed foods, microwave ovens, and food processors to speed up the cooking process. Food preparation, like other elements of the modern lifestyle, must be easy, convenient, and swift. We want to finish it quickly so we can rush to the next item on our busy agendas—eating what we just have prepared.

We usually consume our food at the same frantic pace at which we prepared it, with little or no thought to eating as a sacred act. We eat with the TV blaring or with a newspaper or book in hand. We eat while we work, while we get dressed, and while we drive the car. We will eat wherever and whenever we think it will fit into our schedule.

We pay an enormous price for this attitude about eating, because each time we plow through our food we are telling ourselves that eating is really a nuisance, not an opportunity to savor life. We reinforce the perception that life is too hectic to enjoy each of its various parts. Our life then competes against itself: eating *versus* working, relaxing, reading, gardening, playing tennis, etc. Life in competition with itself is not life; it is only existence.

Creating alternatives

Harriet Kofalk creates alternatives to this perception about food preparation and eating in her center called Peace Place in Eugene, Oregon. She regularly leads "The Peaceful Cook," a cooking class more about centering oneself in the infinitely rich present moment than about culinary procedures. Once the food is lovingly and mindfully prepared at Peace Place, it becomes part of the sacred eating ritual.

The sacred eating ritual that Harriet shares is similar to many eating rituals from traditional peoples around the world. The common denominator is the reverence for the physical and spiritual qualities food contains—something Jesus, Buddha, Thoreau, Gandhi, Native Americans, and others also have emphasized. These two forms of nourishment are always available to anyone who desires them. Before we explore the Peace Place Sacred Eating Ritual, let's consider these thoughts from Harriet's book, *The Peaceful Cook.*

> Food is to our bodies what thoughts are to our minds—the fuel that feeds our soul. By paying attention to our food we create power–full fuel for our bodies; we become reconnected with food as the source of our physical well–being. We can then reconnect with its source—and ultimately our own—in the universe. We begin to understand our place in the continuum of life, as well as to experience the interconnectedness of all creation. We can then digest our food more deeply and use it more effectively, just as we use our thoughts more deeply, more effectively, when we are aware of their focus and aim and interconnection.
>
> Harriet Kofalk, *The Peaceful Cook*

— Peace Place Sacred Eating Ritual —

Preliminary Considerations

• You do not need to perform this ritual at every meal. Our busy schedules preclude that for most people. The goal is to perform it at least once a day when you have the time to center your awareness upon both the cooking and the eating processes. Get into the habit of performing the ritual by celebrating it once a week initially. Its benefits will build momentum and will lead you into regular practice.

• The ritual honors and celebrates the vital life energy of foods from Mother Earth. Use fresh foods—not pre–packaged mixes or frozen dinners—to receive the maximum benefit for your spirit and for your body.

• Celebrate the ritual on Mother Earth Sacred Events (see Mother Earth Calendar beginning on page 142).

1. Once the food is mindfully prepared (see sample food preparation ideas and recipe from *The Peaceful Cook* below), a small portion of the food is placed in a bowl that is covered with a white cloth. The covered bowl is placed in the center of the table.

2. Those partaking of the food sit around the table and silently meditate upon the food in the covered bowl. They honor its source and the spiritual and physical energies it represents. They reflect upon what the food personally means to each of them. They give thanks to Mother Earth for the food she lovingly has provided from her own body.

   This part of the ritual is more than the hurried "saying grace" that some people use as a blessing for the food they will eat. Meditation involves each person deeply and intimately in the food–blessing act, not just the person "saying grace." Meditation also is not a memorized prayer that one repeats each time a need arises. It is a spontaneous experience uniting each person who is meditating with each other and with the food he or she will partake, as well as with Mother Earth and with God as the source of all life.

3. Food in the covered bowl that has been blessed by the group's meditation is then mixed with the other food. This unites the energies of the food that everyone collectively blessed with the food that each person individually will consume. Each person then carries that blessing in their awareness to others after the meal. The blessing ripples outward into life.

4. Participants now consume their food, mindful of its origins and its usefulness to us.

Sample Food Preparation Suggestions and Recipe

Harriet's book *The Peaceful Cook* contains many recipes grouped by the four seasons, along with food preparation suggestions for opening ourselves to the sacredness of the cooking act. Harriet introduces each recipe with an element she calls *The View of the Whole*—something to think about while preparing that dish. This *mindfulness principle* helps us develop the habit of focusing upon food preparation rather than upon other things while we are in the kitchen.

Harriet also includes with each recipe an element called *Embracing Mother Earth*—an Earth–related comment about an ingredient or cooking activity. This element helps us unite our awareness with Mother Earth whose body supplies the ingredients for our recipes and the fuel we use in cooking. The recipe below from Harriet's book illustrates her mindful approach to food preparation.

Tamale Pie

— View of the Whole —

The spiritual significance of cornmeal is almost unknown in Western culture today. To many indigenous people, corn represents humanity with each kernel a human being. As we cook with cornmeal today, we can contemplate this and gain both the serenity of focused endeavor and the joy of another level of meaning to the foods we eat.

2 cups dry pinto or kidney beans
1 Tbsp. cumin

1 1/4 cups cornmeal
2 1/2 cups vegetable stock or water
1 tsp. Bragg's Liquid Aminos (a salt substitute)
1 tsp. chili powder (or more, to taste)
herbs to taste: cumin, basil, oregano, dill, thyme
2 cups fresh seasonal vegetables, chopped
2 Tbsp. tomato paste
1 cup grated cheese

Cover beans with water and soak overnight. Drain and cover with fresh water. Add cumin and simmer 2 1/4 hours or until tender. Meanwhile, mix cornmeal, stock, liquid aminos, and 1/2 tsp. chili powder in a saucepan over medium heat. Stir continuously until mixture thickens and all the liquid is absorbed (about 10–15 minutes). Press mixture into sides and bottom of a buttered 9" x 13" x 1 1/2" deep baking dish, saving 1/4 of the amount to spread on top later.

In a separate pan, combine cooked beans (which can be mashed with a potato masher, leaving some whole) with other ingredients except the cheese. Cook over medium heat until vegetables are almost cooked. Pour into baking pan and spread evenly. Sprinkle grated cheese on top and spoon on remaining cornmeal mixture. Bake at 350 degrees for 25 minutes. Serves 6 to 8.

— Embracing Mother Earth —

Save energy by using glass or Corningware pans that require an oven temperature 25 degrees lower than metal pans. Enjoy!

.   .   .

– John McMurphy

Summer Solstice Celebration

The two Solstices are pivotal points in the year when the Sun shines for the longest (June 21 in the Northern Hemisphere) or shortest time (December 21). Solstices represent a transition from a period of increasing light and diminishing darkness before the Summer Solstice to a period of increasing darkness and diminishing light before the Winter Solstice. The two Solstices are important turning points between the periods of increasing and decreasing light and darkness.

Since the Solstices are turning points in the flow of natural energies necessary for life on Mother Earth, traditional peoples around the world recognize them as a time for us to consider our own natural energies. For thousands of years, people have gathered on these two transition points to become individually and collectively attuned to the flow of Mother Earth's energies. During these occasions, each of us can pause to reflect upon our own lives and the ever–changing flow of natural energies around us and within us.

Summer Solstice: Mother Earth is at her life–creating peak at Summer Solstice. She has brought forth from the creativeness of her womb the beauty of flowers and the bounty of food. By harmonizing ourselves with her natural energies and rhythms through rituals and celebrations, we can focus our energies towards enriching our lives and nurturing our alliance with her.

Summer Solstice also is a time to celebrate one's uniqueness as well as to realize one's unity with others, with Mother Earth, and with God, the Unity in which all things participate. Customary activities include outdoor celebration of rituals, dancing, singing, games, and feasts. If weather permits, conduct the following or a similar ritual outdoors in an open space such as a field or park.

Preparing for the
Summer Solstice Ceremony

1. Read through the ritual several times to become familiar with its theme, content, and activities. The ritual contains prayers and ideas reflecting Christian, Native American, and Celtic traditions. While these elements have been selected to promote the main theme, please use any prayers or ideas you feel are appropriate for the theme.

2. Adapt the activities for the number of people in your group. Have copies of the ritual readings for each person. Use the comments and ideas that are contained within the brackets [ ] to narrate where you feel it is needed.

3. You will need these items for the ritual:

   • Have a central table for your altar with group members seated or standing in a circle around the altar. Decorate the altar with flowers and any other items suitable for the season that you feel appropriate. Use incense (rose, lavender, or other flower essences). Have several candles on the altar to represent the Sun's light.

- You will need a bowl containing flower petals (rose petals, if possible).

- Have a bundle or braid of sweetgrass ready to light for the Invocation.

- You will need a vial of flower oil or essence (rose oil, if possible) for the Anointing.

- Group members should bring an offering of flowers that they will place on the altar during the ritual. Have a few extra flowers in case someone forgets to bring flowers.

Note: Flowers and plants are living beings. If you choose to gather them, be mindful that you are taking their life. If you do gather flowers or other life from Mother Earth, offer prayers and blessings for what you gather, just as traditional people do when they make the choice to gather life from Mother Earth.

PART ONE: Invocation

- The leader lights the sweetgrass. As the smoke rises to the sky, group members place their offering of flowers upon the altar and then form a circle around the altar.

- The leader guides the group through the following prayer and body movements. The group says the prayer in unison.

[Group looks up, raises arms toward the sky and repeats aloud]: Oh, our Father the Sky, we thank you for the light and warmth you send us.

[Group looks down, lowers arms toward Mother Earth, and says aloud]: O, our Mother the Earth, we thank you for the gifts of life you give us.

[Group faces East and bows saying aloud]: We thank you, O Spirit of the East, for your gifts of renewal.

[Group faces South and bows saying aloud]: We thank you, O Spirit of the South, for your gifts of physical well–being.

[Group faces West and bows saying aloud]: We thank you, O Spirit of the West, for your gifts of reflection and vision.

[Group faces North and bows saying aloud]: We thank you, O Spirit of the North, for the clarity you give to our minds.

[Group joins hands and says aloud]: We thank you, O Spirit of the Universe, for your presence in all things.

• The leader lights candles on altar and reads the following passage aloud:

The spirit forces are all around us. They are constantly showing themselves to me and to others who willingly open themselves to the universe.

Sun Bear, *Walk in Balance*

• Group affirms the following aloud:

I am open to the Spiritual Presence in me and in all things around me. I welcome Spirit into this place and into this moment.

Affirmation adapted from Celtic Prayer

PART TWO: Prayer of Consecration

• The leader reads the following prayer aloud:

We should understand well that all things are the works of the Great Spirit, Wakan–Tanka (the One Presence and One Power). We should know that Wakan–Tanka is within all things: the trees, the grasses, the rivers, the mountains, and the four–legged animals, and the winged–peoples...When we do understand all this deeply in our hearts, then we will love and know Wakan–Tanka, and then we will be and act and live as Wakan–Tanka intends.

Words of Black Elk, Sioux Elder

To the Rose—Ancient Symbol of Summer's Beauty and Blessings:

[Flowers symbolize Mother Earth's embodiment of Divinity through their union of beauty and practicality. Flowers not only delight our eyes and noses, they also play an essential role in the propagation of new plant life that also ensures food for animals. Flowers, therefore, reveal Mother Earth's Spiritual Principle that one's nature contains both beauty and practicality.]

• The leader places his or her hands upon the bowl of rose petals on the altar and reads the following poem aloud:

Rose, you majesty—once, to the ancients, you were a calyx with the simplest of rims.
But for us, you are the full, the numberless flower, the inexhaustible countenance.

In your wealth you seem to be wearing, gown upon gown, upon a body of nothing but light; yet each separate petal is at the same time the negation of all clothing and the refusal of it.

Your fragrance has been calling its sweetest names in our direction, for hundreds of years; suddenly it hangs in the air like fame.

Even so, we have never known what to call it; we guess...
And memory is filled with its unawares which we prayed for from hours that belong to us.

Rainer Maria Rilke,
from The Sonnets of Orpheus (Part Two, Number Six)

PART THREE: Blessing & Anointing

• Group members anoint one another on the forehead with flower oil (rose oil, if available).

> —As you anoint someone, say a silent blessing for the person.

> —As you are being anointed, say a silent prayer for Mother Earth and her many forms of life.

• Anointing Mother Earth: When all in the group have been anointed, the leader starts the following litany. The leader reads the first line from the litany. Then, as the group members say aloud their parts, the leader pours a drop of flower oil on Mother Earth (or in a vessel to be poured on Mother Earth later if the ritual is being performed indoors). Repeat until you complete the litany.

Leader: The steep mountains, the roaring oceans, the swift rivers, the verdant fields...

Group in unison: I am one with these blessings.

Leader: The deep blue sky, the radiant Sun, the twinkling stars, the silvery moon...

Group in unison: I am one with these blessings.

Leader: The towering trees, the wind-swept grasses, the fragrant flowers...

Group in unison: I am one with these blessings.

Leader: The rains, the clouds, the storms...

Group in unison: I am one with these blessings.

Leader: The singing birds, the graceful deer, the joyful dolphins, the small hidden animals...

Group in unison: I am one with these blessings.

Leader: Mother Earth, in all the forms she can take as the body of God...

Group in unison: I am one with these blessings. So be it.

Litany Inspired by Navajo Song for Mother Earth

PART FOUR: Thanksgiving & Rejoicing

• The leader reads the following verses aloud:

Praised be You, my Lord, with all your creatures, especially Brother Sun, who is the day and through him You give us light.

Praised be You, my Lord, through our Sister Mother Earth, who sustains and governs us and produces varied fruits, flowers, and herbs.

St. Francis of Assisi,
excerpt from "Canticle of Brother Sun and Sister Moon"

• Each group member now takes a few flower petals from the container on the altar. In turn, each group member will share aloud something for which they are thankful at this moment. After each one shares his or her thanksgiving, he or she joyfully and merrily tosses the petals into the air, letting them fall where they may. After all have shared their blessings, then the leader reads the following passage as a closing prayer:

— Closing Reading —

Oh Great Spirit whose voice we hear in the winds,
And whose breath gives life to the world—hear us.
We give thanks for the light from Father Sky
And for the summer's bounty on Mother Earth.
As we go our separate ways from this gathering,
Help us walk in balance and help our eyes always
See the beauty you have placed all around us.
Help us respect all the things you have made.
We want to learn all the lessons
You have hidden in every rock and leaf.
May we always remember our Unity.

Adapted from a Lakota Sioux Prayer

- The leader extinguishes the candles.

- Continue your celebration with these activities:

    — Play "Ring around the Rosie" or other playful group games.

    — Perform the Cherokee Tree Ritual on page 104.

    — Sing joyful songs, dance, tell stories, play the guitar or flute, and make masks.

    — Use the ideas from the Mother Earth Calendar.

— created by John McMurphy and Jeff Davis

Winter Solstice Celebration

The Sun mesmerized our distant ancestors in the Northern Hemisphere, as they watched it make its annual trek toward the south. Darkness and coldness increased each day of its southerly journey, and it grew more distant and less powerful. It appeared to them that the Sun was "dying."

Then, one day the Sun stopped its death march and hovered in the sky before beginning to move north again, increasing the daily presence of light and warmth. The Sun had died and been reborn! This day–the Winter Solstice–was a time for celebrating the Sun's victory over death and its rebirth from the "Cosmic Womb." Our ancestors learned that light and dark—birth and death—are not opposing forces, but are complementary forces which are part of life itself.

Through time, the Sun's annual death and resurrection became significant in most world mythologies. The following stories are examples:

• **Christianity**—Jesus, born from Mary's "Cosmic Womb" at the Winter Solstice, becomes the light of the world who dies and is reborn. Early Christians celebrated the Winter Solstice as one of their most sacred holidays.

• **Egyptian Mysteries**—It is Osiris who dies and is reborn through the power of Isis' blood. At the Winter Solstice, celebrants carry lamps in a procession to celebrate the resurrection of his light.

• **Northern Europe**—The Solstice was celebrated at many sacred sites such as Stonehenge. Crowds gathered while the priestesses helped the Sun attain its rebirth from the "Cosmic Womb."

• **Native Americans, Africans, and Asians**—Virtually all cultures in the Northern Hemisphere celebrate the annual death and rebirth of the Sun at Winter Solstice. In the Southern Hemisphere, similar rituals are performed at Summer Solstice when the Sun dies and is reborn. Winter Solstice is one of humanity's most ancient rituals. Its basic message is that we need not fear darkness or death, because these are balanced with light and birth in the web of life on Mother Earth. Life and death are part of the *process* of life.

Suggestions for the Winter Solstice Ceremony

1. Read through the ritual several times to become familiar with its theme, content, and activities. The ritual contains prayers and ideas reflecting world religions and cultures, including Christianity, Hinduism, Buddhism, Celtic, Native American, and Confucianism. While these elements have been selected to promote the main theme of the interrelatedness of light and dark, use any prayers or ideas you feel are appropriate for the theme.

2. Adapt the activities for the number of people in your group. Have copies of the ritual for each person. Use the comments and ideas that are contained within the brackets [ ] to narrate where you feel it is appropriate.

3. The items needed for the ritual are listed on the next page. Have a central table which will be your altar with group members seated or standing in a circle around the central table. Use incense (myrrh, holly, cedar, etc.) if you like.

- A large red or yellow candle in the center of the altar table to represent the Sun

- A candle for each participant

- A container of seeds (beans or any large seed)

- A container of soil for planting seeds

PART ONE: Invocation

• Group leader lights central candle on the altar which represents the Sun.

• Leader reads aloud: [Centering Prayer]

We should understand well that all things are the works of Wakan-Tanka, the Great Spirit (the One Presence and One Power)...Peace comes within the souls of people when they realize their relationship, their oneness with the universe and all its powers, and when they realize that at the center of the universe dwells the Great Spirit, and that this center is really everywhere, it is within each of us.

Black Elk, Sioux Elder

• Group reads aloud in unison: [Unifying Prayer]

Let us be united;
Let us speak in harmony;
Let our minds apprehend alike.

Alike be our feelings;
Unified be our hearts:
Common be our intentions;
Perfect be our unity.

From the Rig Veda, an ancient spiritual text from India

PART TWO: Celebrating the Unity of Darkness and Light

• Group members, in turn, light their candles from the central candle. If there is a large crowd, then the leader lights the candles of a few people who pass the light on to others.

• When all candles are lit, the leader reads the following two poems aloud [In Hindu myths, Kali is the Goddess who weaves light and dark into ONE; she teaches us that light and dark—like life and death—are not opposites but are complementary parts of the Universal Oneness]:

> Kali, be with us...
> Help us to be the always hopeful
> Gardeners of the Spirit
> Who know that without darkness,
> Nothing comes to birth
> As without light, nothing flowers.

excerpt from poem by May Sarton

To know the dark, go dark. Go without sight, and find that the dark, too, blooms and sings, and is traveled by dark feet and wings.

excerpt from "To Know the Dark" by Wendell Berry

• Group extinguishes candles **one-by-one with an oral reflection** on a loss (a lost/departed opportunity, friend, relative, relationship, etc.) they may have experienced during the past year. They also should reflect upon what they have learned or could learn from the loss.

• Leader exits the room with Sun candle [explain that this symbolizes the annual "death" of the Sun]. While the Sun is gone from their presence, group members reflect **silently** for a few minutes upon the loss each one selected. After a few minutes of silent reflection upon the loss, the leader returns with the Sun candle [symbolizing the annual "re–birth" of the Sun] and places it in the center of the group.

• Group, in turn, re–lights candles from central candle. As each person lights his or her candle, they affirm aloud the words of Confucius:

"It is better to light one small candle than to curse the darkness."

• After all candles are re–lighted, the leader reads aloud the following passage:

Not all forms are physical. A thought, for example, is a form. What is a thought formed out of? A thought is energy, or Light, that has been shaped by consciousness…You are a dynamic being of Light that at each moment informs the energy that flows through you. You do this with each thought, with each intention.

Gary Zukav, *The Seat of the Soul*

• Group members reflect silently upon the "seed thoughts" (the thoughts, words, or actions) they have sown this year which support "light" (e. g., seeds of peace, justice, kindness, joy, or love) and what has "sprouted" from these seeds.

[PAUSE for a few minutes so each person can reflect upon the "seed thoughts" of light he or she has contributed this past year. After a few minutes of silent reflection, each person takes a seed from the seed container.]

• With their seed from the container in their hands, group members then reflect silently for a few moments upon the "seed thoughts" of light they would like to plant for next year.   [PAUSE for a minute or two.]

• Group members, in turn, share aloud what "seed thoughts" they would like to sow during the coming year. After sharing aloud their "seed thoughts," then participants plant their seeds in the soil and cover their seeds up with soil.

• After all seeds are planted, group **in unison** affirms aloud the words of Jesus:

I am a light for the world.

PART THREE: Blessing of Compassion

• Group reads aloud in unison these words:

If anyone has hurt me or harmed me knowingly or unknowingly in thought, word, or deed, I freely forgive them. And I too ask forgiveness if I have hurt anyone or harmed anyone knowingly or unknowingly in thought, word, or deed.

May all beings be happy. May all beings be peaceful. May all beings be free.

excerpt from the Buddhist "Loving Kindness Meditation"

PART FOUR: Departing Blessing

• Leader starts with first sentence, and each participant in order reads one sentence. [Adjust as is necessary for the number of people in your group.]

May the blessing of light be upon you, light without and within.

May the blessed Sun shine on you and warm your heart till it glows like a great peat fire, so strangers may come and warm themselves at it.

May the light shine out of your two eyes, like a candle set in the windows of a house, bidding the wanderer to come in out of the storm.

May the blessings of Mother Earth be on you, the great round Earth.

May the Earth be soft under you when you stop to rest upon it.

May the Earth rest easy over you when at the last, you lay out under it.

May the Earth rest so lightly over you that your soul may be off from under it quickly and be on its way to God, the Unity of all things.

May God bless you all and bless you kindly.

Adapted from a Traditional Celtic Prayer

Suggestions for celebrating the Winter Solstice include the following:

• Light a Yule Log.

• Share refreshments appropriate for the season.

• Tell stories and sing songs beside the fireplace.

• Make wreaths and garlands from greenery.

— created by John McMurphy and Jeff Davis

PART FIVE
Mother Earth Resources

- ***Mother Earth Sacred Calendar***

- ***Mother Earth Sacred Sites in North America***

- ***Mother Earth Sacred Symbols***

- ***Mother Earth Organizations***

Mother Earth Sacred Calendar

◊ JANUARY ◊

— Movable Feasts and Celebrations —

Makara Sankranti is a festival in India to celebrate that the Winter Solstice has passed and to welcome the increasing daily light and warmth.

◊ FEBRUARY ◊

1 & 2   Cross–quarter or Imbulc Festival

The Earth is Mother of all that is natural.

She is mother of all,
for contained within her
are the seeds of all.

All creation comes from her depths.

Hildegard of Bingen

This ancient Mother Earth festival on February 1 & 2 (evening of the 1st and day of 2nd) is known as Cross–quarter Day, because it is the halfway point between the Winter Solstice and the Spring (Vernal) Equinox. The Celtic people called it Imbulc or Imbolg. At this time of the yearly cycle, days are getting noticeably longer, and the Sun grows stronger. Also at this time, Mother Earth is readying herself deep within her womb for the new life she soon will bear.

Ritual activities included singing songs of praise and thanksgiving to Mother Earth while circling the gardens and fields where the crops and flowers would later grow. The circling movement is always done as follows: move from east to south to west to north to create a large circle. Repeat the circle.

This resembles the path the Sun takes on its daily journey and is a way for us to unite Father Sky's movements with Mother Earth's movements. Building bonfires along the edges of the circle or carrying candles while circling the fields symbolized the return of light (the Sun).

Significance: At Cross–quarter Day/Imbulc, winter is slowly fading as the days get longer, brighter, and warmer. Deep in her womb and hidden from our view, Mother Earth is preparing herself for the new life she will bear in a few weeks. We can direct our awareness toward the needs of Mother Earth at this turning point as she prepares to bring forth new life. We also can offer thanks to God, the Divine Creative Intelligence, as source for the coming renewal in Mother Earth.

Activities: This is a time for putting winter's darkness and cold behind us and for beginning the transition to spring. One tradition is the burning of winter greenery used during the winter holidays and celebrations (see Winter Solstice celebration). If you saved some of the holly, fir, cedar, pine, mistletoe, etc., you can burn these now to help prepare for spring's "greening."

Another ancient tradition is to take branches of greenery and place them along the pathways in your garden. The acidic nature of evergreens helps deter unwanted plants from growing along the pathways. Later, in spring, remove the branches.

You also can prepare your garden for spring in the ancient manner by circling (see circling note above) or by walking around your garden as you offer prayers and affirmations focusing upon renewal and regeneration of life.

Affirmations:

- I make way for the renewing powers of spring in and around me.

- I welcome the renewal of life in Mother Earth.

- I give thanks for the unity of all life in God.

◊ MARCH ◊

2 1   **Spring (Vernal) Equinox**

A single raindrop
as the newly–opened apple blossom
takes in spring
stays with me
the whole day
creates memories from moments
that sparkle in the brief sun
between showers

Harriet Kofalk

Spring Equinox marks one of the two days each year in which there is an equal amount of light and dark (the Autumnal Equinox is the other). From the Spring Equinox until the Summer Solstice in the Northern Hemisphere, days will be longer than nights, a condition necessary for Mother Earth's growing season. The reverse is true in the Southern Hemisphere.

Since light and warmth have overtaken the dark and coldness at the Spring Equinox, Mother Earth now beckons to the slumbering life within her (seeds, roots, animals, etc.) to awaken for their renewal. In Greek mythology, Persephone is now preparing to return from the Underworld to her mother Demeter. Demeter, likewise, is preparing to renew life on the surface to celebrate her daughter's return from the Underworld.

Spring also embodies what twelfth–century mystic Hildegard of Bingen called *Viriditas*—the greening power of God. *Viriditas* was a divine word to Hildegard that expressed God's unlimited creativeness as source for life on Mother Earth. She even referred to God as "the purest spring."

Significance: Mother Earth is becoming more active within her "womb," as seeds begin to release their stored life energy, as roots and bulbs trigger new growth on the surface, as fruit trees blossom, and as animals begin new families. The Spring Equinox also is a date in which the Sun rises due east. Historically, in Mother Earth traditions, the east represents wisdom, enlightenment, and the influx of light into our lives.

Respect for this ancient Mother Earth tradition led Solomon to build the Temple in Jerusalem on an axis aligned with the Spring Equinox. Nearly all Mother Earth cultures had temples, shrines, or sacred sites in which the light from the Sun falling upon Mother Earth's body at the Spring Equinox was a day for great celebration and reverent worship. On this day, we can join our brothers and sisters in honoring Mother Earth's renewal process and its relationship with light.

We also can focus upon our need for making the psychic transition from winter to spring, just as we make the transition from autumn to winter at Samhain/Halloween (see October). Mother Earth is becoming more active each day in her efforts to provide for life, and we can follow her lead. We can prepare to give birth to new "life" (awareness, love, justice, art, joyfulness, or ideas) as we become more active during the months ahead. Remember, we are creative partners with Mother Earth and with God.

Activities: Spend time in your garden or nearby park or nature preserve observing Mother Earth's "awakening" processes (buds appearing or opening, early spring flowers, birds building nests, etc.). As you observe each awakening process, give thanks to her and to God, the ultimate source of all the awakenings that are now happening on Mother Earth. Continue observing and offering thanks for Mother Earth's awakening processes until you feel attuned to her creative powers of renewal and regeneration.

When you return home, read and open yourself to the creative energies expressed by poets and writers in the Poetry and Sacred Verse Section of this book, as well as the writings of others inspired by Mother Earth. Jot down your response to their ideas. Also, reflect in your journal upon your personal impressions of Mother Earth's creative energies you experienced while in the park or garden. Meditate upon your experiences and focus upon the renewal of energies you personally will need in making the shift from winter to spring.

Begin sprouting plants for transfer to your garden after the last frost. If appropriate in your climate, plant seeds or seedlings outside now (see the Sacred Planting Ritual on page 107). Bless with prayer as you place them in Mother Earth, both the seeds you gathered from last year's plants and those seeds or seedlings you may have purchased. As you plant the seeds or seedlings, try to experience yourself as the seed or seedling. Feel your intimacy with the soil as you make each planting. Acknowledge and give thanks for your kinship with all life on Mother Earth.

Throughout Europe, one ancient symbol for the Spring Equinox has been the egg. Eggs represent the potential for new life, an essential characteristic of this Mother Earth holiday. In the Ukraine, people dye and decorate eggs to exchange with friends. Use natural dyes such as beet juice, tea (regular and colored herb teas like Red Zinger or Blackberry), turmeric, and onion skin. Decorate the eggs, if you like. In Italy, people bake loaves of bread with hard-boiled, peeled eggs inside for themselves and to share joyfully with others as gifts.

Affirmations:

* I welcome light into my life.

* I give thanks for my oneness with all life.

* I celebrate the renewal in and around me.

◊ APRIL ◊

5   Buddhist Feast of Kuan Yin

All things are of one pattern made;
Bird, beast, and plant,
Song, picture, form, space, thought, and character,
Deceive us, seeming to be many things,
And are but one.

Ralph Waldo Emerson, excerpt from "Xenophanes"

Kuan Yin is the ancient Great Mother Goddess in China, the embodiment of the Yin Principle (she is *Kwannon* in Japan). When Buddhism came to China over a thousand years ago, she was so important in the Chinese psyche that she became part of Chinese Buddhism. April 5 is the day she reminds us of the Buddhist principle of *karuna*—Boundless Compassion for all life on Mother Earth.

Significance: Buddhists celebrate our capacity to have compassion for all forms of life on this day. They recognize that all life is sacred and is interrelated. By focusing our awareness on this one day to the sacredness and interconnectedness of all life, we will enhance our capacity to have compassion for all life throughout the year.

Activities: Explore your relationships with the animals sharing your home and garden. Open yourself to their being, like you, manifestations of the Divine Unity we call God. Also open yourself to experience the sacredness of all the animals and plants you encounter on this day. Spend as much time as possible on this day meditating upon your capacity to have compassion for all life.

Affirmations:

• I honor all life as an expression of God.

• All life is sacred, and all life is interconnected.

• My compassion for all life is boundless.

13   Cerealia—Roman Thanksgiving

Joy is a garden
delight
in every sense
simply
being
eating
the fruits of our labors
we share
the sweetness
with every smile.

Harriet Kofalk

Ceres is the Latin equivalent of the Greek Goddess Demeter or Earth Mother. In the Roman world, she was part of the Trinity of Goddesses: Juno, the Queen of Heaven, Prosperine, the Goddess of the Underworld, and Ceres, the Great Earth Mother. Farmers around the Mediterranean regarded her as the source of food, and they honored her with a festival each year. On this day they gave special thanks to their Earth Mother for the foods she provides throughout the year.

Activities: In the Mediterranean, Cerealia is one of the many days to offer thanks to Mother Earth for her fruitfulness. You might find the Sacred Eating Ritual on page 120 a meaningful way to honor this thanksgiving tradition. Also, reflect upon Harriet Kofalk's poem "Priorities" on page 91.

2 2   ## International Earth Day

Since 1972, people all over the world have focused upon our need to honor Mother Earth and to protect the environment. Most communities have activities in which you can participate. Refer to the Mother Earth Organizations Section beginning on page 207 to locate national and local groups observing Earth Day activities. Honoring Mother Earth on this day reminds us of the reverence we need towards her everyday.

— Movable Feasts and Celebrations —

Arbor Day (last Friday in April) in the U.S. and **Kalpa Vruksha** in India (date varies) are days for honoring trees. Suggestion: Use the Cherokee Tree Ritual on page 104 and Planting Ritual on page 107.

◊ MAY ◊

1   ## May Day/Beltane/Floralia Festival

> Praised be You, my Lord,
> through our Sister Mother Earth,
> who sustains and governs us
> and produces varied fruits,
> colored flowers, and herbs.
>
> St. Francis of Assisi,
> from "Canticle of Brother Sun and Sister Moon"

May Day/Beltane is one of the most important days in the Celtic/Northern European Mother Earth calendar. May Day is another Cross–quarter Day, because it is halfway between the Spring Equinox and the Summer Solstice. Mother Earth is "greening herself all over" as mystic Hildegard of Bingen might say. The Roman world also celebrated the day as Floralia, a day honoring Mother Earth's flowering during the spring.

Significance: May Day is a day for honoring the importance of Mother Earth's "flowering" as a Spiritual Principle. Flowers are not only beautiful expressions of life just as they are; they also are necessary parts of the life cycle. Flowers eventually wither, and most become the fruits and vegetables that animals consume or the seeds for new life in coming seasons. The apples, pears, squash, and beans that we eat were once flowers. Flowers epitomize the dynamic interplay between beauty and practicality that we find throughout Nature.

As we consider our tasks in life, we can look for the interplay of beauty and practicality in our own lives. This awareness may help us create a new perception of the tasks we may not cherish (for example, washing dishes, changing a diaper, painting the fence, or balancing our checkbook). Every task has its own beauty—if we open ourselves to it. Beltane/May Day/Floralia is a day to celebrate the interplay between beauty and necessity as a Spiritual Principle in Nature that we can employ in our own lives.

Activities: Celebrate flowers and flowering. Spend time amidst flowers, either in fields, parks, or in your garden. Explore their world and how it can help you with yours. What wisdom do flowers have that they would like to share with you? Use your senses and your imagination—both of which are powerful resources we can use to explore this glorious world in which we live.

Note: Flowers and plants are living beings. If you choose to gather them, be mindful that you are taking their life. If you do gather flowers or other life from Mother Earth, offer prayers and blessings for what you gather, just as traditional peoples of the world do when they make the choice to gather life from Mother Earth.

Weave a few strands or garlands of flowers. Wear one and use others as decorations. Another "flowering" tradition is the May Basket. Use small straw or cane baskets, or you may make baskets from paper or other recyclable materials. Decorate with ribbons, if you like. Fill them with fresh flowers to give to loved ones and friends.

Another ancient tradition to celebrate May Day is the May Bowl filled with May Wine. In early May, the herb sweet woodruff that is traditionally part of May Wine should be available. Legends say that sweet woodruff increases our merriment. Please make certain that any herbs or flowers you will ingest are edible and have not been sprayed with pesticides or other harmful chemicals. A recipe for May Wine—with and without alcohol—follows:

10 to 15 sprigs green–dried* sweet woodruff – or –
1/3 cup dried packaged sweet woodruff
2 tablespoons sugar (optional)
2 .750 liter bottles sweet white wine – or –
1/2 gallon of apple juice (or white grape juice)
Juice of 1 or 2 lemons
1/2 pound sliced fresh strawberries
1 bottle champagne – or – 1 liter of seltzer water

Directions: Steep the sweet woodruff overnight with the sugar in two cups of the white wine or apple juice if you prefer an alcohol–free libation. Strain. Add the rest of the wine or apple juice and the lemon juice to taste. Pour over a block of ice in a punch bowl, and add the strawberries and the champagne or seltzer. If possible, gather fresh sweet woodruff blossoms and use them as a garnish on top of your punch bowl containing May Wine.

> *Note: To green–dry sweet woodruff, place sprigs of it in a large earthenware bowl or wide–mouth glass jar. Cover with a dry cloth, and leave for two days.

Traditionally, we offer the first cup of May Wine to Mother Earth as a sacred libation. Offer a blessing such as: "We thank you Mother Earth for bringing into our lives the beauty and the practicality of flowers. We know your flowering is an expression of your creativity. Please accept our gratitude." Take the cup and pour its contents upon Mother Earth. When you have poured the libation upon Mother Earth, drink your own portion. If you perform the ceremony indoors, pour the wine into a container that will be offered to Mother Earth later.

Affirmations:

- I celebrate flowering in my life.

- I honor the unity of all life on Mother Earth.

- I celebrate life as a union of beauty and practicality.

— Movable Feasts and Celebrations —

Shavout is an ancient Hebrew harvest festival that falls fifty days after Passover.

◊ JUNE ◊

21   Summer Solstice

In spite of all the farmer's work and worry
he can't reach down to where the seed is
slowly transmuted into summer.
The earth bestows.

Ranier Maria Rilke,
from The *Sonnets to Orpheus*

Summer Solstice, the longest day and shortest night of the year (just the opposite in the Southern Hemisphere), is another opportunity to celebrate the interplay of light and dark as part of life. Mother Earth uses this interplay to create and to nurture life. Both are necessary for life to exist, and we can respect both as ingredients of life. From now until the Autumnal Equinox, darkness will slowly overtake light as the days grow shorter and nights longer.

Significance: Summer Solstice is a time for celebrating Mother Earth's balance and harmony as she brings forth life. Life celebrates itself during summer.

Activities: Join Solstice celebrations in your community, if available. If not, create your own or use the one provided in this book (see page 126). Other suggestions for celebrating include the following: spend *mindful* time in Nature, experience the sunrise and sunset, feed animals in your garden or a park, and perform the Cherokee Tree Ritual (page 104) and/or the Native American Sunrise Ritual (page 102).

Affirmations:

• I celebrate both light and dark as elements of life.

• I welcome the dark that now increases each day.

• I give thanks for life and its abundance.

◊ JULY ◊

— Movable Feasts and Celebrations —

Green Corn Dance is the day the Seminole people celebrate to honor the first harvest of their corn crop. Corn is one of the sacred foods for the Seminole and other Native Americans, including the Hopi, Navajo, Pueblo, and Iroquois.

◊ AUGUST ◊

1 **Lammas/Lughnasadh**

> To everything there is a season,
> a time for every purpose under the sun...
> A time to be born and
> A time to die,
> A time to plant and
> A time to pluck up that which is planted.
>
> Ecclesiastes Chapter 3

Lammas/Lughnasadh marks the end of the growing season in northern portions of the world. The summer grasses that are cut as hay for the livestock are now being gathered and placed in storage. Wheat and barley, two important foods for humans and other animals, are almost ready for harvest. In Ireland, this is the time to start digging up the new crop of potatoes. Lammas is a day for celebrating Mother Earth's summer abundance by gathering for feasts and dancing, for holding contests and games, and for marriages.

Lammas also is a season in which Mother Earth begins to withdraw her life-giving powers in preparation for winter. Seeds are ripening on plants. Those not harvested for eating or for planting next year will fall to the ground. If Mother Earth were still active and creating new life, the seeds falling upon her body would sprout and be killed by the coming winter frosts. The withdrawal of her life-creating energies at this time is necessary to ensure an abundance of life next season.

Significance: As noted above in the ancient Mother Earth wisdom found in the Bible's Book of Ecclesiastes, life is a cycle of birth, blooming, and death. All life on Mother Earth experiences this cycle. What lives and blossoms also will die.

Lammas and other Mother Earth traditions remind us that we should not fear death as the end of life. Life and death are not opposing forces that battle with each other. Life and death are one; they are part of the *process* of being alive. The cycle of life includes both birth and death. The circle of life is a Spiritual Principle operating throughout Mother Earth and her many life forms.

At this time of the year we start to see Mother Earth moving her energies away from creating new life. The timely ending of life is necessary for the *process* of life to continue. At this time of the year, we can affirm the circle of life as a Spiritual Principle. We can honor our lives in their fullness—as a unity of birth, blossoming, and death.

Affirmations:

- I celebrate the cycle of life as a Spiritual Principle.

- I give thanks for the *process* of life.

- I give thanks for the unity of birth and death in the circle of life.

— Movable Feasts and Celebrations —

Choosuk or Moon Festival in Korea is held to celebrate the beginning of the harvest. People come together with what they have harvested to bless it as a gift from Mother Earth.

Onam in India is a harvest festival with themes similar to Lammas.

◊ SEPTEMBER ◊

22   Autumnal Equinox

> As I become
> a part of the garden
> breathing with the apple tree
> listening to the pears ripen
> opening petal after petal
> of my being
> I encompass
> more
> of the patterns of growth
> the gentle guidance
> that moves the seasons

and the sun
in their rounds
that are my rounds
that are eternity
viewed from the dewdrop
in its fullness
and my own

Harriet Kofalk, "Autumn"

As in the Spring Equinox, there are equal amounts of light and dark on this day. Winter's gusts of cold air begin moving down from the north to replace summer's warmth. Mother Earth is fully engaged in preparing for winter. Harvesting nears completion, and food for the coming winter is being prepared for storage.

Significance: As another day in which light and dark play a role in the cycle of life, we can participate in traditional activities to celebrate their interplay. We also can pause to reflect upon the life–giving foods that summer provided, many of which are in storage for the coming winter.

Activities: Arise to watch the sunrise and take time to watch the sunset. Offer prayers at both of these occasions for the sacred interplay between light and dark. Autumn's exchange of light for darkness prepares both Mother Earth and ourselves for winter. Gather plants, flowers, roots, herbs, and leaves today that you will dry to use as decorations in your home until the spring renewal offers new decorations. Remember to honor what you gather.

Affirmations:

• I welcome the dark as part of life itself.

* I give thanks for the bounty summer provided.

* I focus upon the light within me as the nights grow longer and the days grow shorter.

◊ OCTOBER ◊

10   **Canadian Thanksgiving Day** is when Canadians join other cultures to celebrate their many blessings and Mother Earth's fruitfulness.

31   **Cross–quarter Day/Samhain/
All Hallow's Eve/Halloween**

> Emerald
> gold
> copper and bronze
> day by day
> she turns the ring
> of her seasons
> winding it
> on the fingers
> of her land
> until
> taking a breath of cold air
> she disrobes
> and then puts on
> a gown of purest white
> sprinkled with diamonds
> in which to dream
> of seasons
> yet to come...

Harriet Kofalk, excerpt from "The Ring"

Samhain is the Celtic Cross–quarter Day between the Autumnal Equinox and the Winter Solstice. Fields lie dormant, the harvest has been stored, and Mother Earth is taking a much–needed rest.

Samhain celebrations honor Mother Earth's bounty. They also are important to help people psychologically prepare for the coming of winter. This is a crucial time for us in the cycle of life as we must adjust from a period of summer's energetic outdoor activities to winter's cold and darkness and its quieter indoor orientation.

Another dimension of the holiday comes from the ancient belief that the boundary between the mortal world and the world of spirits becomes delicate at this time. Spirits of ancestors now may return to the earthly plane to visit their kinfolk who still are alive. In ancient days, people had gifts and trinkets on hand to give their ancestors' spirits should they manifest. This practice led to the trick-or-treat custom of present-day Halloween. The Catholic Church, as with other Mother Earth sacred days, later "Christianized" Samhain as All Saints Eve with All Saints Day falling on November 1.

Significance: Our ancestors did not take the annual transition from summer to winter lightly. They understood the human psyche well enough to recognize that we must shift both our physical and our psychic energies just as Mother Earth is shifting her energies. Celebrating Samhain gave psychic closure to the summer and helped our ancestors adjust to the daily increases in darkness and coldness. Perhaps they understood the potential for Seasonal Affective Disorder (chronic depression during the winter when there is less light) that affects many contemporary people. We can use this ancient wisdom and the holiday that employs it to help us make the necessary psychic transition from summer to winter and from outer to inner.

Activities: Walk in your garden or in a park or nature preserve and notice how Mother Earth has made closure upon her summer activities (birds migrating, dry seed pods, dry leaves, squirrels busily storing nuts, etc.). As you discover one of her closure activities, give thanks to Mother Earth for it and to God as the Unity in which all things participate. Continue observing and giving thanks until you feel spiritually in tune with Mother Earth's closure process. When you return home, meditate upon the closure activities you personally will need for the transition from summer to winter. Reflect upon the energies you will need for the coming winter and how these energies differ from those you needed in summer.

Have a traditional Samhain/Halloween Festival: bob for apples, make treats to exchange with friends and loved ones, decorate your house with dried flowers, leaves, herbs, and the fruits, nuts, and vegetables of the season such as pumpkins, acorns, gourds, squash, and corn.

In the spirit of Samhain/All Hallow's Eve, place candles in windows to honor your departed loved ones. Review photo albums in which your departed loved ones appear. Give thanks to the contributions they have made to your life. Open yourself to their continuing presence in your life.

These joyful activities help us put psychic closure on the summer and help us prepare for the winter, as well as honor our ancestors. They also are important parts of the seasonal transformations all animals and plants undergo. Allowing ourselves to be part of Mother Earth's rhythms and cycles will enhance our experience of life.

Affirmations:

- I give thanks for creating closure in my life.

- I welcome the shift in life energies at this season.

- I welcome winter as a time to explore my inner world.

- I honor my departed loved ones (use their individual names).

— Movable Feasts and Celebrations —

Sukkot is a Hebrew harvest festival that evolved from ancient Near Eastern Mother Earth traditions.

◊ NOVEMBER ◊

— Movable Feasts and Celebrations —

Thanksgiving in the U. S. started in New England where Native Americans shared their late autumn "giving of thanks" ritual with the newcomers from Europe. Most cultures around the world celebrate at least one day each year as a special day to give thanks to Mother Earth and to God as the Unity of all things; however, they also practice *thanks–giving* every day.

◊ DECEMBER ◊

21   Winter Solstice

Winter Solstice is the longest night and shortest day of the year. Since the Summer Solstice, the waning Sun has slowly been moving south, and days have been growing shorter. From now until next summer, the dark's reign in the Northern Hemisphere diminishes daily as days gradually grow longer. Winter Solstice is the last of the many Mother Earth's holidays (in the cycle of the calendar year) centered upon the interplay of light and dark.

Significance: Winter Solstice is a special time in many European/Mediterranean religions. Light's "victory" over dark has translated into holidays such as Christmas and the Mystical Re–birth of Osiris in Egypt.

Activities: Refer to the Winter Solstice Ritual in this book (page 134). Perform the Cherokee Tree Ritual (page 104) and/or the Native American Sunrise Ritual (page 102).

Affirmations:

• I welcome light into my life.

• I am filled with light.

• I share my light with others.

• It is better to light one small candle than to curse the darkness.   (Confucius)

• I am a light for the world.   (Jesus)

— John McMurphy

North American Mother Earth Sacred Sites

We are affected by streams of varying potency issuing from the earth.

Plutarch, *The Decline of Oracles*

Sacred space makes possible the communication with transcendent realities...Every consecrated space represents an opening towards the beyond, towards the transcendent.

Mircea Eliade, *Symbolism, the Sacred, and the Arts*

Anthropologists tell us that every culture they have come across, both ancient and modern, has sacred sites that serve vital functions within the culture's spiritual life. The sacred site usually is a valley, cave, stream, mountain, or other area left in its natural state. We often construct temples, altars, or shrines at these natural sites and consecrate them as sacred space. Whether it is a natural area or a place we have built, a sacred site unites Mother Earth with Transcendent realities.

According to mythological and spiritual traditions from various cultures, we have not chosen these sites to be sacred; Mother Earth has chosen them. She has chosen certain places in her body to make her spiritual energies readily available to help us transcend our earthly needs and priorities so we can communicate directly with her, with our ancestral spirits, and with God as source. Her sacred spaces also allow our shaman, priests and priestesses, and mystics to journey between different dimensions of existence.

Sacred space is where Mother Earth teaches us her ways, the ways to live in harmony with her and with all her many lifeforms. Mother Earth's sacred sites also empower our rituals and ceremonies with the spiritual energy that helps us attune ourselves to the natural rhythms around us such as the cycles of the Moon and Sun and the changing seasons.

Mother Earth's sacred sites also help us heal ourselves when we become ill. Even Christianity which does not openly acknowledge Mother Earth as sacred realizes that certain places on her body such as Lourdes or Chimayó are healing sites.

For these reasons, Mother Earth's sacred sites play significant roles in every element of our spiritual lives. They are as important for our spiritual well–being today as at any time during our long presence on the planet. Visiting these sacred sites and opening ourselves to Mother Earth's energies can inspire us to attain the peace and harmony in our lives that we intuitively know is possible. These are Mother Earth's natural ways, and she is patiently waiting for us to listen and to learn.

Note: The sacred sites listed in this section are ones that I have visited and can recommend to you as places in which you may experience Mother Earth speaking. There are many other North American sacred sites not mentioned where Mother Earth can speak to us.

— Suggestions for visiting sacred sites —

1. **Be aware of your surroundings:** Sacred sites are part of the natural eco–system that we may injure simply by our visiting them, even when we are careful. Remember to leave no sign of your visit and to take nothing with you from the

site except your experience and photographs, sketches, or journal entries, if appropriate.

2. Be reverent of your surroundings: You are visiting a sacred place. These North American sites—many of which have become state, provincial, or national parks—are as sacred to Native Americans as the Notre Dame Cathedral or the Wailing Wall in Jerusalem might be to those with European religious heritage. Many sites remain important sacred sites to Native Americans, even though the area may seem to be just another park or historic site. Please maintain reverence for the unique spiritual energies at the site, no matter where it is located.

3. Be one with your surroundings: Native Americans are drawn to these sites by their awareness of the spiritual energies running through Mother Earth and of the gathering of these energies in sacred sites. These energies are part of the *spirit of the place* important to Native Americans. Meditate at the site to open yourself to these energies and to hear Mother Earth speaking. Use your journal to record any insights that may emerge. The goal is to become one with the sacred energy within and around you.

— Sacred Sites in Canada —

Ontario: Petroglyphs Provincial Park

Four hours north of Toronto is an extraordinary example of reverence for Mother Earth. Ontario's spectacular Petroglyphs Provincial Park, located amidst tall timbers and pristine mountain streams, contains Algonkian petroglyphs (rock carvings) at a site the Algonkians call the "teaching rocks."

This sacred site, characterized by its large weathered outcroppings of limestone, is so sacred to the Algonkians that only certain members of the community are allowed to visit it. For several hundred years, this has been the site they use to teach the next generation of shaman the "facts of life"—reverence for Mother Earth and her hidden creative powers.

Elder shaman bring initiates to the petroglyphs to teach them how to enter Mother Earth's sacred belly and to become one with her energies. The rock carvings offer the initiates a visual tutorial of a sacred truth:

> The Ontario Petroglyphs carved on top of natural openings in the rock are each a symbolic uterus and a means of access to the hidden spiritual powers of nature into which the shaman journeys.

Sacred Art of the Algonkians by J. & R. Vastokas

The petroglyphs found here unite human creative efforts with Nature's creative efforts, an important principle to Native Americans. Natural crevices and openings into the rock surface are symbolic openings into the body of Mother Earth. Each is a symbolic uterus or entry point that leads into the mysterious creative powers of Mother Earth.

The Algonkians carved symbols around these natural openings into Mother Earth's body to illustrate their reverence for her life–giving and life–sustaining powers. Their creation blends harmoniously with that of Mother Earth herself, as all of our actions can.

These symbolic openings in Mother Earth's body, just as the uterine opening in a woman's body, are points of great power and are sacred. Within both the bodies of Mother Earth and of women—her human partners—is the sacred power to create and to nurture life.

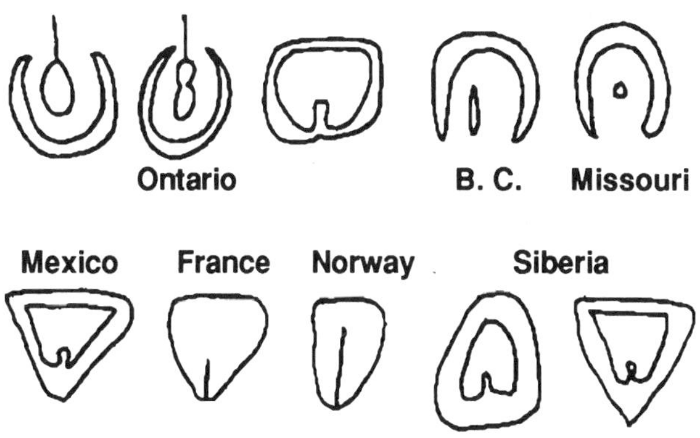

Drawings of petroglyphs from various locations illustrating reverence for Mother Earth's and for a woman's natural capacity to create life.

Reverence for the creative powers of Mother Earth and of her human partners is certainly not limited to the Algonkians. Numerous cultures across great spans of time and space have carved symbolic uteri into rock openings to show respect for life itself. The drawings above, made from my research into petroglyphs created by different cultures, illustrate the widespread reverence for Mother Earth and for women. Notice their resemblance to the opening into a woman's body and to her hidden creative powers.

The carvings in Petroglyphs Provincial Park are among the most eloquent testaments we have to the profound reverence for Mother Earth—and for *woman* as her human partner—that radiates throughout human experience. Approach the site with awe and remain open to the unique voices Mother Earth uses at this sacred site. The Algonkian still use the petroglyphs as "teaching rocks."

In the magnificent Provincial Park where the petroglyphs are located, you can spend an entire day (or days) visiting the sacred site, exploring hiking trails, and meditating beside streams and lakes. There is a visitor center with an excellent video program on the petroglyphs and other materials.

Directions: Take the 401 from Toronto to Newcastle where you take 115 to Peterborough. From Peterborough take 28 North for about 25 scenic miles. Watch for the Provincial Park signs at which you turn right for another 10 miles. Signs will direct you to the park entrance and to the short hiking trail to the petroglyphs. The park is day–use only and is open from May through October.

Petroglyphs Provincial Park
General Delivery
Woodview, ON K0L 3E0 Canada
(705) 877–2552

— American Sacred Sites —

Arizona: Sedona Energy Vortices

Sedona's sacred energy is most discernible, even through the commercialism and trendy boutiques that have taken root there. You *feel* the energy as well as *see* it embedded in the majestic red mountains towering along Oak Creek Canyon.

For many centuries, Sedona has drawn Native Americans to the area for rituals, healing, and spiritual renewal, because there are four distinct energy vortices present in Mother Earth. A vortex is a location where energy will flow naturally either upwards from Mother Earth (called a masculine vortex) or downwards into her body (a feminine vortex). Masculine energy flowing upwards from a vortex is physically and spiritually stimulating and uplifting. Feminine energy flowing downwards into Mother Earth provides centering and receptiveness to our own inner world. Sedona is one of the few places on Earth that has all three of the different vortex types.

- The Bell Rock Vortex and the Airport Mesa Vortex are masculine in nature.

- The Cathedral Rock Vortex is feminine.

- The Boynton Canyon Vortex contains both masculine and feminine energy.

Visit each of the three types to experience the unique energies that can flow through Mother Earth at a vortex. Meditate and open yourself to the energy at each site. Vortex maps are available throughout Sedona.

Directions: From Phoenix, take I–17 north to the exit marked for Sedona. Travel time from Phoenix is about two hours. A visitor's guide is available from the address on the next page.

Sedona Chamber of Commerce
Route 89A
Sedona, AZ 86336
(602) 282–7722

Note: Located about an hour south of Sedona is visionary architect Paolo Soleri's *Arcosanti* community. Soleri and his associates are constructing a community using ancient Mother Earth wisdom. *Arcosanti* eventually will be home for five thousand people living harmoniously with Mother Earth. There is a guided tour and educational opportunities such as Elder Hostels and work–study programs. I–17 to Cortes Junction and follow the signs.

Florida: Crystal River Archaeological Site

One of North America's most ancient sacred sites is on Florida's Gulf Coast about 80 miles north of Tampa. From around 200 BCE through about 1400 CE, a mound–building culture thrived along the beautiful and tranquil Crystal River. Their mounds pre-date the more widely known mounds of the Hopewell and Mississippi Mound Builders along the Ohio and Mississippi River Valleys.

The Crystal River Mound Builders, like several other Southeastern mound building people, flourished for many centuries and then mysteriously vanished shortly before Europeans arrived. While much remains a mystery to us about these people and their way of life, their mounds testify to their intimacy with Mother Earth.

At Crystal River, the temple and burial mounds—two distinct types of mounds found in mound cultures—are accompanied by two large stelae or stone slabs inscribed with symbolic images. These stelae resemble ones found in the Mayan culture of Central America. The stelae and the mounds at Crystal River were built for a sacred purpose, as were the mounds Native Americans built in other Mother Earth sacred sites.

The mounds and stelae are "earth" objects created to align precisely with "sky" objects (Sun and stars) on certain sacred dates: Winter and Summer Solstices and Spring and Fall Equinoxes. Alignment between Mother Earth and Father Sky helped create balance and harmony in the lives of many Native Americans.

Toltec Mounds in Arkansas

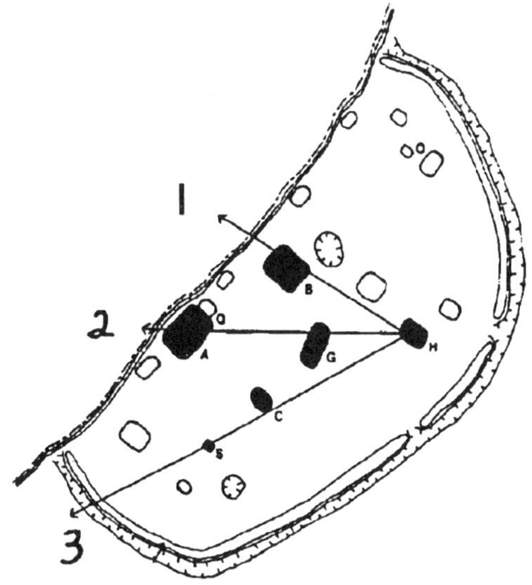

These mounds, like the ones at Crystal River and other mound sites, unite Mother Earth with Father Sky. The mounds allow the people within the mound complex to experience this relationship at four important events: (1) Sun alignment with mounds at Summer Solstice (2) Sun alignment at the Spring and Fall Equinoxes (3) Sun alignment at Winter Solstice. Mound H is the main temple mound used in all four ceremonies.

Crystal River has a visitor center and museum with exhibits and a video program to help visitors understand the significance of this ancient sacred site. Well–marked trails lead you on a tour of the mounds and stelae. Markers illustrate the Mother Earth principles by which these sacred objects were built. The tall mound adjacent to the river is an excellent place to meditate and to open yourself to the spirit of the place.

Directions: The site is located just outside the town of Crystal River, about 80 miles north of Tampa. Signs along US Highway 19 will direct you to the State Park Road leading to the site. The grounds and museum are open daily from 9 AM to 5 PM. Bring a picnic lunch and spend the day in this beautiful sacred site. Note: Bring citronella or other natural mosquito repellent.

Crystal River State Archaeological Site
Crystal River, FL 32629
(904) 795–3817

Other Significant Mound Sites

While Crystal River is my favorite mound site of the many I have experienced, I heartily recommend the following sites as significant examples of how mound builders revered Mother Earth. Each site contains similarities with other sites. Yet, each is unique, because Mother Earth's subtle energies express themselves differently in various locations. Meditating or opening yourself to the energies present at each of the different sites will reveal the subtle differences that drew Native Americans to a particular site.

Alabama: Mound State Monument
Moundville   (205) 371-2572

Arkansas: Toltec Mounds Park
near Little Rock   (501) 961-9442

Florida: Indian Temple Mound
Ft. Walton Beach   (904) 243-6521

Georgia: Etowah Mounds
near Cartersville   (404) 387-3747

Illinois: Cahokia Mounds Historic Site
near Collinsville   (618) 344-5268

Louisiana: Poverty Point Mounds
near Monroe   (318) 926-5492

Ohio: Hopewell and Adena Mounds
across Ohio   (614) 297-2300

Wisconsin: Aztalan Mound Historic Park
near Madison   (608) 873-9695

New Mexico: Santuario de Chimayó

Long before Europeans arrived in New Mexico, Native Americans frequently gathered at an ancient sacred site now called the Santuario de Chimayó. The indigenous people knew Mother Earth could bring health to them at this site.

The small Catholic Church built at Chimayó sits on top of the ancient Native American sacred healing site. The church quickly learned why the site was important to the people from whom they had taken it. The healings continued for the newcomers, as Mother Earth offered her blessings to anyone who sincerely asked for them at this site. Chimayó soon became known as the "Lourdes of America."

A small chamber adjacent to the church testifies to the healings that occur here regularly. Casts, wheelchairs, braces, canes, walkers, and trusses fill the walls and shelves. Fastened to many of these no–longer–needed objects are hand–written notes of thanksgiving. "Miracles" some people call the healings that occur here. These are not "miracles"—occurrences that transcend the Laws of Nature. They are the Laws of Nature *in operation* for anyone who understands them.

Directions: Chimayó is about 10 miles east of Española, NM and is an hour's drive from Santa Fe. Take scenic Route 76 from Santa Fe towards Taos to Chimayó. The Santuario is at the far edge of town.

Santuario de Chimayó
P. O. Box 235
Chimayó, NM 87522
(505) 351–4889

New York: Ganondagan State Historic Site — Seneca People's "Place of Peace"

For many centuries before the Europeans arrived, the Seneca People lived in harmony with Mother Earth at a beautiful site southeast of Rochester named Ganondagan or "Place of Peace." The Seneca were the most numerous and westernmost of the five Native American tribes comprising the Iroquois Confederacy—the world's first true "league of nations" dedicated to peace and justice. Ganondagan (also known as Gannagaro) was one of the Seneca's most important sacred sites because of their commitment to the way of peace.

The Seneca were forcibly removed from Ganondagan in 1687. The land came under European control, and settlers' plows swiftly obliterated its peaceful heritage. Archaeologists and historians discovered the Seneca's earlier presence in the 1920s, and several decades later it became a historic landmark. Today, the site offers us an opportunity to experience the Seneca's beacon of peace that shines brightly through the spirit of the place.

There are two trails to give visitors access to the Seneca's reverence for this site and for the way of peace they practiced. The Trail of Peace presents Seneca history and traditions. It illustrates how the Seneca and their neighboring tribes formed the Iroquois Confederacy to create and maintain peace and to live in harmony with Mother Earth.

The Earth is Our Mother Trail introduces visitors to the sacred relationship between the Seneca and Mother Earth's plant life. It describes the wisdom the Seneca obtained from paying attention to Mother Earth and how the Seneca used this wisdom in providing food for themselves, in healing, and in spiritual ceremonies.

Allow several hours to saunter along the trails. Pause often and open yourself to Mother Earth's voices that drew the Seneca here. A visitor center with artifacts and educational materials provides additional learning experiences.

Directions: Ganondagan is near Rochester. Exit 44 from the New York Thruway (I–90) to Route 332 South. Go south on 332 to second traffic light. Turn right (west) on County Road 41 which becomes

Boughton Hill Road. Proceed to caution light and cross intersection. The parking lot is the second driveway on the right after the caution light. The Visitor Center is open from Memorial Day through October. Monday through Saturday 10 AM to 5 PM. Sunday, 1 to 5 PM. Trails are open year round (weather permitting) from 8 AM to sunset. You also may want to visit the Seneca—Iroquois National Museum in Salamanca, NY. (716) 945–1738.

Ganondagan State Historical Site
1488 Victor–Holcomb Road
Victor, NY 14564
(716) 924–5848

Texas: Enchanted Rock State Natural Area

Enchanted Rock is a mammoth pink granite rock protruding upwards from the rolling Texas Hill Country west of Austin. The mountain–like rock contains massive amounts of quartz crystal embedded in the granite that contributes to the site's incredible beauty and to its enchantment.

To Native Americans who journey to Enchanted Rock, this is a doorway to the spirit world. Shaman enter through this doorway and visit the Other World. Many Native Americans have found it a suitable place for a vision quest. The Apache believe the Great Spirit sent the spirit *Gan* to live here and to teach the Apache how to live. The energy that has drawn the Apache and other Native Americans to the site still is present.

Directions: Enchanted Rock State Natural Area is about two hours west of Austin. From Austin, take US 290 West to Fredricksburg. From Fredricksburg, go north on Farm Road 965 about 14 miles to the site. Open all year. Camping areas.

Enchanted Rock State Natural Area
Route 4 Box 170
Fredricksburg, TX 78624
(915) 247–3903

Wyoming: Big Horn Medicine Wheel

Built almost thirteen centuries ago on top of the highest mountain peak for many miles, Big Horn Medicine Wheel is a sacred site created to unite Mother Earth with Father Sky so the people would live in peace and harmony. The alignment of the stones into a wheel and spoke pattern reflects complex astronomical relationships celebrated at the Solstices and Equinoxes. Big Horn is the most impressive of the numerous Native American medicine wheels and is among their most sacred sites. Today, it draws tribes from throughout North America for ceremonies.

Directions: Take U. S. Highway 14A east from Lovell, WY or 14A west from Burgess Junction, WY though the Big Horn National Forest. Turn north on Park Road 12 (gravel) to the designated parking area. Intrepreters will greet you at the parking area. You will walk one and one–half miles (slight climb) to the Medicine Wheel where guides will introduce you to the Wheel. Bring a jacket or sweater, and call ahead for weather conditions.

Medicine Wheel Ranger District
P. O. Box 367
Lovell, WY 82431
(307) 548–6541

Wyoming: Mato Tipila (Devil's Tower)

One of the most magnificent sacred sites in North America is the place Native Americans call *Mato Tipila* or "Bear Lodge." The Lakota and their neighboring tribes tell different myths about the origins of *Mato Tipila*. While each tribe's story is unique, each story has at least one common theme—this is a sacred place on Mother Earth. So sacred is *Mato Tipila* that the different tribes in the area have allowed each other to use the site for vision quests and rituals.

Even in modern days *Mato Tipila* beckons that we draw near. Stephen Spielberg's mythic movie *Close Encounters of the Third Kind* focuses upon *Mato Tipila* as the site to which the main characters are drawn by the alien beings. It also is the site chosen by the aliens to initiate contact with humans. Such cross–cultural (and perhaps cross–planetary) fascination with *Mato Tipila* shows our potential for enchantment with Mother Earth. She has much to communicate to us, and *Mato Tipila* is one of her most eloquent voices.

Directions: *Mato Tipila* (Devil's Tower National Monument) is in northeastern Wyoming, not far from South Dakota's two sacred sites—the Black Hills and the Badlands. To reach *Mato Tipila*, exit from I–90 at Sundance, WY. Take US Highway 14 northwest to the monument site. Open all year.

Devil's Tower National Monument
Devil's Tower, WY 82714
(307) 467–5370

— Other Mother Earth Sacred Sites —

While I have not personally visited the sacred sites below, my research and my conversations with people who have visited these sites suggest that they also offer excellent opportunities to experience the sacredness of Mother Earth.

Ontario: Serpent Mound Provincial Park

Perhaps the northernmost mounds that Native Americans built were in Canada. Ontario's serpentine mound, like the related serpentine mound in Ohio, is a sacred space. The serpent is a sacred animal that symbolizes Mother Earth wisdom to Native Americans and to most of the world's peoples. Mounds built to resemble a serpent's body demonstrate Native American reverence for Mother Earth and her wisdom.

This serpent mound unites Mother Earth with Father Sky, just as do other Native American mounds. Mound patterns suggest the people celebrated rituals at certain important dates in the their agricultural and spiritual calendar.

For information —
Serpent Mounds Provincial Park
Keene, ON K0L 2G0
(705) 295–6879

New Hampshire: Mystery Hill (America's Stonehenge)

Near North Salem, New Hampshire is an ancient sacred site that is, as its name suggests, mysterious. Located near the beautiful Merrimack River of which Thoreau spoke fondly, the site contains several large stone monoliths protruding from Mother Earth and arranged in a definite pattern. The same pattern exists in other cultures throughout the world who are intimate with Mother Earth (Stonehenge in England and Big Horn Medicine Wheel in Wyoming are examples).

The monoliths' pattern creates a precise alignment between Mother Earth and Father Sky at the two Solstices and two Equinoxes. Many people attribute the monoliths to Native Americans. Some link the monoliths to Celtic adventurers who sailed here before Columbus. Others say the Phoenicians created the monoliths long before Jesus was born. Yes, a few say space aliens created them. Regardless of their origins, Mystery Hill appears to be another sacred site in which Mother Earth has played a prominent role in human experience.

For information —
Stonehenge on Mystery Hill
P. O. Box 84
North Salem, NH 03073
(603) 893–8300

New Mexico: Chaco Canyon

Chaco Canyon in northwest New Mexico is the site of an incredible sacred complex built by the ancient Anasazi people. Roads that extend for several hundred miles were giant arteries interconnecting the various parts of their complex. Pueblo Bonito, one of the main areas within their complex, used sophisticated architectural principles that integrated the Sun's movement with Mother Earth's movement to create natural heating and cooling (for a contemporary example of this Mother

Earth wisdom, see the note about *Arcosanti* in the Sedona entry above). Anasazi housing, kivas, and roadways contain intricate patterns that reflected considerable astronomical wisdom.

Anasazi petroglyphs and symbols, as well as legends from neighboring people, tell us that the Anasazi were peaceful by nature and maintained reverence for Mother Earth in their way of life. Legends say that Mother Earth drew the Anasazi to Chaco Canyon to learn how to live peacefully and harmoniously. People who have experienced Chaco Canyon often find it difficult to express adequately the depth of their experience at this sacred site.

For information —
Chaco Canyon National Historical Park
Route 4, Box 6500
Broomfield, NM 87413
(505) 988–6716

— John McMurphy

Mother Earth Sacred Symbols

Please consider the following insights on the role that symbols can play in experiencing intimacy with Mother Earth:

The great function of symbols is that they "open up levels of reality which otherwise are closed, and they open up levels of the human mind of which we otherwise are not aware."

Paul Tillich, *Theology and Symbolism*

Symbolic images become devices for extending the mind beyond the boundaries of logical thought. The symbol invested with psychic energy has transformative power.

Frances Vaughan, *Awakening Intuition*

Marie Von Franz paraphrases Carl Jung on symbolism: We cannot know ourselves until we start to live the symbolic life.

Marie Von Franz, *Interpretation of Fairy Tales*

The distinctive thing about the human species is that we are a symbol–making animal...We not only have a capacity for making symbols, but we also *must* create them in order to cope humanly with our experience.

Lynn White, *The Frontiers of Knowledge*

Suggestions for using symbols

• Use the symbol suggestions that follow to help you celebrate Mother Earth Sacred Events. Find and use symbols that help you express themes for the different events. Use the guide for selecting symbols that follows the symbol listings. The guide illustrates how to use symbols and symbolic actions to express your intentions.

• Include symbols in rituals and ceremonies you create to honor significant events in your life such as new beginnings, transitions, births or deaths, and accomplishments or attainments.

• Use symbols as part of your personal altars—the ones inside your home and in your garden.

• Create your own symbolic expressions. If an object suggests a particular meaning to you, then use that object as a symbol in your ceremonies.

Mother Earth Sacred Symbols

Almond: Because of its resemblance to the opening to the womb in a woman's body, many cultures regard it as a feminine symbol of great power. It also symbolizes Spiritual Truth (the meat) which is hidden inside a shell (material life), just as Truth lives at the center of our own being.

Alpha and Omega: The first and last letters of the Greek alphabet. Because they surround the other letters, they are a symbol in Western religions of God's omnipresence and Jesus as the being first and last (i.e., the one and only). Long before this term became prevalent in Christianity, however, an ancient temple dedicated to Isis in Egypt had a similar inscription to indicate that Isis was the beginning (*Alpha*) and the end (*Omega*).

Christianity liked the concept of *beginning* and *end* as a symbol of wholeness and perfection and borrowed it from the Isis worshipers. Think of it as meaning "Spirit is everywhere, throughout Space—Time and beyond." Use Alpha and Omega as symbols of omnipresence, universality, unity.

Apple: In the East, an apple symbolizes peace, and an apple blossom symbolizes feminine beauty. In other areas, apples are an ancient love symbol, particularly a red apple. Because of its spherical form that symbolizes "wholeness," it can be a sign of eternal life and perfection. In Celtic traditions, it is a symbol of spiritual knowledge.

Arc: Arcs are "incomplete" circles (circles represent spiritual unity and wholeness); therefore, arcs symbolize a spiritual principle or reality that has the potential to manifest in the earthly plane of existence. The arc's position indicates its significance:

In the position below, the arc represents the capacity to receive or to hold something spiritual. A cup or chalice is an example.

$$\cup$$

In the position below, the arc represents the inability to receive or to hold something spiritual, something inert, lifeless, or dead.

$$\cap$$

In the following positions, the arc symbolizes something in a state of delicate balance. It may fall one way to become the receiver of Spirit or the other way to become inert and lifeless.

$$)($$

Bamboo: Bamboo, in its natural habitat in the East, is an evergreen plant; therefore, it symbolizes immortality and longevity. The Chinese words meaning "bamboo" and "to pray" are homonyms, indicating a reverence for it. Easterners respect bamboo's essential nature: the joints, individual segments, and its straight stalks symbolize in Buddhism and Taoism the path and individual steps of spiritual development. The bamboo plant also brings good fortune.

Beans: As seeds, they represent "essence of life." They are "keys" to the future. In the very early spring, Hopi elders go down into a kiva, a sacred underground chamber accessible by a ladder. Here they symbolically plant bean seeds in the ground. They pray that Mother Earth will respond by bringing forth many healthy plants and will bless the people in the coming year. In Japan, beans symbolize happiness, good fortune, and fertility. In the Pythagorean Mystery Rites, eating beans was a sacramental act. (*see Seed*)

Bell: Bells are associated with "mysteries" and contact between ourselves and spirits. In many sacred images from the Mother Earth cultures, bells often formed the body of a Goddess. Her head would have been the handle used to ring the bell. In the East, the bell symbolizes the connection between heaven and Mother Earth. In China, the ringing of the bell symbolizes the cosmic harmonies. In Islam as in Christianity, the sound of bells is considered to be an echo of the voice of God. When you hear a bell, its resonating sound carries the soul beyond the secular world into the spiritual world.

Book: Books symbolize intellectual freedom and knowledge. Opening a book during a ceremony symbolizes opening ourselves to intellectual knowledge. Consider using books to represent the intellect (*logos*) in conjunction with almonds or apples to represent inner, intuitive wisdom (*gnosis*) to achieve balance in your ceremony.

Bread: Bread not only nourishes our physical body, it also is thought to nourish the soul. In the mystery traditions of Egypt, bread is associated with the body of the god Osiris who dies and is reborn. As a sacramental act, worshipers ate bread to symbolize eating Osiris' body to obtain immortality. The Greeks also used bread to symbolize the body of Dionysus, their deity who dies and is reborn. Christianity, following the lead from both these earlier Mediterranean mystery rites, also uses bread as the "body" (the Host) of its resurrected deity Jesus. In many other cultures, bread symbolizes the union of our physical needs and our spiritual needs.

Bread, made from grains, also symbolizes Mother Earth and her fecundity. In many ancient cultures, the Goddess was also known as *Grain Mother*, the one who gives us our daily bread, our essential nourishment. The breaking of bread symbolizes a bonding between people or between ourselves and some idea, principle, or pledge we make.

Candle: The light or flame is masculine energy that penetrates darkness or feminine energy. Thus, a candle unites light (masculine) with dark (feminine) creating wholeness, balance, and unity. The sacred interplay between light and dark is universal, and burning candles is one of our most cherished spiritual acts. Lighting or extinguishing a candle or lamp may signify the birth or death of a person, of an idea, or of a new reality.

Cave: As an opening into Mother Earth's body resembling the opening in women's bodies, caves have been feminine symbols since prehistoric times. During the Ice Age, caves "nurtured" us by keeping us safe, dry, and warm relative to the life outside caves. Carl Jung says we have a deep archetypal relationship with caves the way we have with our own mothers. That is why they are a frequent place for the initiation "re–birth" experiences in the ancient Mediterranean Mother Earth Mystery Religions. Celebrating rituals in caves or creating a cave–like atmosphere for rituals deepens the experience, because of our archetypal associations with the Mysteries of Life.

Cedar: As an evergreen, it symbolizes immortality. Its towering height symbolizes lofty and sublime things. Its wood is durable, making it a symbol of strength and endurance. Its aroma suggests earthiness, groundedness. Ancient Near Eastern cultures considered cedar groves to be oracular shrines, a place for meditation and revelation.

Cherry: The cherry is associated with the feminine capacity for creating life (blood). In Japan, cherries also symbolize self-sacrifice (the giving to others of our essential nature) by its red/blood color.

Chrysanthemum: In China and Japan, chrysan-themums symbolize long life. Its name in

Chinese is related to the words meaning "long time" and "to remain."

Circles/Spheres: Circles and spheres represent Mother Earth, her fullness, unity, and harmony. Circles also are a symbol for the Oneness of the Universe, the Universal Intelligence found in all things. In all parts of the earth, circles are used to create a sacred space so that all things inside the circle are one with each other and with the universe itself (Stonehenge, Native American ceremonial gathering sites, Hindu shrines, etc.).

Container: Containers are powerful feminine symbols, because they receive and hold things and thus frequently are a symbol for the womb and its generative powers. Whatever we place within the container (for example, a seed–thought written on paper, another symbol, or an offering) is brought to life by the womb–like qualities of the container. *(see Cup/Chalice)*

Cord: Its most ancient association is with the human umbilical cord, the binding of infant to mother. In Mediterranean Mystery Religions, cords were used to help prospective initiates find their way back to Mother Earth's "Cosmic Womb" where they could be reborn as enlightened beings. Initiates, often blindfolded or in natural darkness to resemble the birth canal, used their hands to follow cords to the sacred chamber or cavern underground which represented Mother Earth's womb. A cord is also an image of connection or binding. Tying a cord into a knot binds or seals a promise or a reality that you desire to manifest.

Corn: One of the four sacred plants to many Native Americans (e.g., Hopi, Navajo, Seminole, Pueblo, and Iroquois) and a highly valued nutritional plant. Corn symbolizes abundance, well-being, and happiness—all natural blessings that spring from Mother Earth when we walk the balanced path of life. Corn also represents humanity: each kernel represents a person, and the kernels united together on the cob represent humanity as a whole. Refer to the corn–based recipe in the Sacred Eating Ritual beginning on page 120 and the Navajo Corn Prayer on page 119. (*see Seed*)

Cowrie Shell: The cowrie is most likely humanity's most ancient spiritual symbol. Its first use as a spiritual symbol occurred during the Ice Age where it was placed in burial sites, perhaps to suggest "re–birth" of the departed one because it resembles the "Portal of Life" through which humans emerge from their mother's body. In Africa, it is one of the most frequent symbols for abundance and for the psychic "death and re–birth" humans experience during rites of passage such as initiations, marriages, and menarche.

Cross: The cross is one of humanity's most ancient and universal symbols. The cross has many levels of meaning. First, the cross is a graphic symbol for the Four Sacred Directions on Mother Earth's body. The cross also is a union of two realities: the vertical line or axis represents Spiritual Reality— the spiritual dimension of the universe; the horizontal line represents Earthly Reality—the physical or natural dimension of the universe. From this perspective, the cross indicates our dual realities: we are Spirit, and we are Nature.

In rituals, the cross reminds us of our need to balance our spiritual needs and priorities with our physical needs and priorities. This gives us the balance we need to lead the lives for which we were created. We are both Spirit *and* Nature.

Crystal: Crystal symbolizes purity, clarity, and spiritual reality. The crystal ball used as a focusing of awareness into spiritual or Transcendental reality most likely originated among the Druids.

Cup or Chalice: A symbol for the womb of which it bears resemblance. It also is a container, another important feminine symbol (*see Container*). Cups elevated in a toast are uniting Mother Earth (her blood in the cup is the grape or grain used for wine, ale, or libation) and Father Sky. Thus, elevating a cup in a toast is an act of binding or sealing a reality, making it important in many ceremonies. Cups can also represent abundance and overflowing of life. Cups can represent the physical body (the cup chamber itself) which houses the spiritual body (the contents of the cup, usually wine, the "spirit" of the grape).

Dawn: In the Isis Mysteries, the redness of the dawn was a sign that the blood of Isis had been successful in resurrecting the Sun from its "death" (sunset). Dawn is a sign of new life and new beginnings, a symbol of hope. Ceremonies at dawn draw upon the powers of the new life emerging in the day (See Native American Sunrise Rituals on page 102).

Door, Gate, or Portal: A door symbolizes transition from one realm to a new one. Examples include:

transition from this life to others, from one level of consciousness to others, from one state of being to another, and from the ordinary/temporal to the sacred/infinite. In ancient India, the vulva was the "Holy Door of Birth." Moving through a doorway in a ceremony indicates transition and movement.

Egg: As the starting point for life, it is a widely recognized symbol of new beginnings. It also symbolizes abundance of life. In China, eggs are given to people who are ill so they may give birth to a recovery. The Chinese dye eggs red (associated with blood and therefore new life) to give to others at New Year. Use eggs to help celebrate Spring Equinox (*see Mother Earth Calendar*).

Fire: Fire is masculine energy of action and transformation from one state of existence to another that is associated with the Sun. Use fire to liberate or transform realities (e. g., burn a piece of paper with an obstacle you now face or feel you may face written upon it or light a candle as a symbol of moving past an obstacle). *(see Candle, Light, and Sun)*

Fish: As a Water element, fish symbolize life and fertility. In China, the word for fish and the word for abundance are phonetically related, so fish are a symbol of abundance and prosperity.

Fruit: Fruit is a symbol of completion (ripeness), of bringing an activity or phase of life to an end. It also symbolizes Mother Earth's abundance and bounty. Figs, peaches, apricots, and pomegranates are generally feminine symbols. Fruits with many seeds are a fertility symbol. *(see Pomegranate)*

Gems: As hard, durable, sparkling rare minerals that can be polished or ground to shape, they represent "terrestrial stars," which are images of the heavenly light of truth on earth.

Gold: It is a symbol of immutability, eternity, and perfection. Because of its color, it also has been universally identified with the Sun or fire.

Hammer: Hammers are a masculine symbol for power and strength. It is *doing* energy.

Hand: The human hand is a symbol of activity and power. Verbs in Mayan hieroglyphs were created to show some activity taking place in the palm of a human hand. Hands represent *doing*.

Hand and Foot Washing: In almost all religions people wash (especially their hands) before holy actions as a sign of purification. In addition, footwashing is a sign humbling oneself to the spiritual presence within other people.

Hat: Associated with the head, hats symbolize thoughts or thinking. Changing hats may also signify changing one's views or opinions or changing one's occupation or role.

Heart: As a vital, central organ in humans, it is associated with the symbolic meaning of the center. Today the heart generally symbolizes love and friendship.

Honey: Often associated with milk, it represents sweetness, gentleness, or the highest earthly or heavenly good, and hence the condition of perfect bliss (*Nirvana*).

Horn of Plenty: The Horn of Plenty (Cornucopia) is a symbol of *Fortuna*—the personification of autumn and is a symbol of good fortune and a rich harvest.

House: In the East, as a planned, enclosed area, it symbolizes cosmic order. It is a strong feminine symbol and can represent the womb.

Ivy: Like other evergreen plants, it symbolizes immortality. Ivy's nestling and snuggling characteristics made it an ancient symbol of friendship and fidelity. In ancient Greece it was given to brides and grooms at weddings as a sign of their union. Ivy often was used in Druid rituals.

Key: The symbolic meaning of the key has to do with its power both to open (create new realities) and to lock (seal or move beyond old or outgrown realities). In the symbolic language of Mediterranean Mystery Traditions, possessing a key often signifies the condition of one's being initiated.

Kiss: Probably originally perceived as the breath of the soul, it was also thought of as transferring power and as life-giving. The kiss is usually an expression of spiritual devotion and a sign of reverence.

Knife: As a sharp cutting tool, it symbolizes the masculine or active principle. In rituals, a knife can be used to symbolize cutting through barriers and obstacles along one's path.

Knot: Tying a knot is a symbol of linking, bonding, or the connection to protective powers, as well as an indication of complications and obstacles in one's path. Untying knots is a sign of overcoming obstacles. *(see Cord)*

Lamp: *(see Candle and Light)*

Lemon: In Judaism, lemons symbolize the human heart. In the Middle Ages it was regarded as a symbol of life and was used as protection against forces that threaten life (i.e., against magic spells, poison, pestilence). As a seedy fruit, lemons are fertility and prosperity symbols.

Light: Light, thought by many to be the essence of the universe, is a common symbol for Transcendence, Spirit, and God, but also for life and happiness.

Lily: In the East, the day–lily is known as "the plant that helps you forget your troubles." The white lily symbolizes light, purity, and innocence.

Lotus: Many different water lily flowers are known as lotus that plays a significant role in the East. At sunset it closes its blossom and retires for the evening into the water. At sunrise the blossom re–opens, which makes the Lotus an ancient Sun or light symbol. The white, blue, or red blossoms that rise out of murky water also symbolize purity overcoming impurity. In Buddhism, the lotus is one of the Eight Precious Things.

Milk: As human's first food, it symbolizes fertility, spiritual and intellectual nourishment, and the nurturing of life.

Mirror: It symbolizes knowledge, especially self-knowledge, as well as truth and clarity.

Mistletoe: Druids use mistletoe as a preventative against illness, lightning, and magic spells, and to bring good fortune. As an evergreen, it symbolizes eternal life.

Money: Money represents Spiritual Energy active on the physical plane.

Oils: Many cultures view oils as the bearers of special powers, and oils are used in anointing people with those powers. Oils also are used in healing ceremonies. Because the olive tree bears abundant fruit on poor soil, its oil symbolizes spiritual power and is especially honored in many cultures.

Orchid: In the East, people place orchids (kin to lilies) in a vase to symbolize concord and harmony.

Pearl: Pearls are lunar and feminine symbols. In China it is closely associated with the moon, water, and woman, and the Yin principle. In ancient days in China, a pearl was placed in the mouth of the deceased to symbolize rebirth, new life. Because of its spherical form and its incomparable luster, the pearl also is a symbol of perfection.

Pine: *(see Cedar)*

Pomegranate: Like other fruits with many seeds (*e.g.,* pumpkin, gourd, lemon, orange, tomato), it is a fertility symbol. In Greek mythology, Persephone ate six seeds from the Pomegranate which bound her to the Underworld for six months each year. *(see Fruit)*

Rainbow: It is a symbol of the connection or union between heaven (see Sky) and Mother Earth and in China between Yin and Yang.

Ring: As a shape without beginning or end, it represents eternity. It also symbolizes joining, fidelity to, or membership in a particular group.

River: Close in meaning to Water, its flowing nature is not only a symbol of time and temporality but also of perpetual renewal. The union of rivers with the oceans symbolizes the union of the individual and the absolute. *(see Water)*

Rock: Rocks symbolize solidity and steadfastness.

Room (Chamber): A feminine symbol as it suggests the womb or a grave (a place where one type of life experience "dies" and a new life experience is born). In many initiation rites it was common to place the initiate in a secret room, chamber, or subterranean space to represent the maternal womb or the grave. *(see Cave)*

Rose: One of the most frequent feminine mystery symbols used in religions around the world. In Asia, roses are the "Flowers of the Goddess." In the Gnostic mystery tradition, the menarchal blood of *Psyche*–the Virgin Soul–causes the first rose to appear. Roses are important Christian symbols to represent the blood of Jesus. The Rose Window of cathedrals represents the Virgin Mary. Red roses often are presented at menarche to the new initiate as a symbol of her womanhood. Roses are used in Summer Solstice rituals to celebrate Mother Earth's flowering activities (See the Summer Solstice Celebration beginning on page 126).

Salt: Highly valued because of its role in health and its scarcity in earlier times, it symbolizes vitality and is used for warding off misfortune. In the Middle East, salt is used for consecrating an altar.

Sand: Sand symbolizes infinity (along with Stars) because of the infinite number of grains of sand.

Scissors/Shears: *(see Knife)*

Seed: A seed is a symbol for the essence of life and for the abundance of possibilities not yet developed. The seed that "dies" in Mother Earth so that a plant may sprout is a symbol of Mother Earth's transformational and renewal powers. Seeds also signify sacrifice, as well as the spiritual rebirth of humankind. *(see Bean)*

Sesame: Asians regard sesame seeds as a food that prolongs life and strengthens the spirit; therefore, Sesame represents longevity and spiritual nourishment. *(see Seed)*

Sieve: It symbolizes sorting out of alternatives and separation and differentiation among various realities.

Silver: It is the "Moon Metal" that symbolizes the moon and its powers. As a shiny white metal, it also is a symbol of purity.

Sky: In many ancient religions, the sky (*AKA*, Father Sky) and Mother Earth were equal in importance and were "wedded" to each other in sacred marriage celebrations throughout the cycle of the year. In later patriarchal religions, however, they are "divorced," and the sky begins to play a superior role in Western mythological and religious conceptions. In these religions, the sky is believed to be the place from which invisible gods and divine beings (*Yahweh*, *Baal*, etc.) exert their powers over humanity and to which the soul rises after death (heaven). Symbols for sky include Sun, air, birds, feathers, etc.

Smoke: Smoke unites heaven (see Sky) with Earth and spirit with matter. Many Native Americans use the smoke of sweet grass to unite Mother Earth and Father Sky in their ceremonies. In China, smoke symbolizes transitory matters, realities that change and evolve according to unseen spiritual principles.

Snake: A powerful symbol of wisdom and transformation in ancient cultures. Snakes are a feminine symbol in most ancient traditions. The snake also has been a symbol of immortality since it renews itself by shedding its skin regularly. In the Arabic language, the words "snake," "teachings," and "life" are closely related. To the Celtic people, Mother Earth's wisdom sprang up from her body in the form of a snake and wrapped itself around a person to provide wisdom.

Spiral/Labyrinth: Since Neolithic times, the spiral has been a symbol for the generative powers of Mother Earth and the feminine capacity to give life. They symbolize the journey of life, death, and rebirth. Spirals have become labyrinths, a constructed reality that one traverses to symbolize penetration into Mother Earth's womb (in Christianity the journey is to find God) and rebirth again with her wisdom.

Square: In many ancient Mother Earth religions, the square represented the four corners of the Earth and the four sacred directions (N, S, E, and W). In Christian art the square represents the Earth as opposed to the half sphere of the sky. The square is a frequent element in sacred geometry and is used as the floor plan for many ancient temples. The square represents stability and a lack of change whenever it is used.

Stairs: Ascending a set of stairs symbolizes emotional and spiritual development and gradual, "step–by–step" gains in wisdom or knowledge. Descending a set of stairs symbolizes gaining access to the realm of the dead, to esoteric knowledge, or to the unconscious.

Stars: In many ancient cultures, stars represented angelic beings or spiritual light penetrating the darkness. The movement of the stars in fixed patterns across the sky symbolizes harmony in the cosmos which is important in astrology.

Sun: The Sun is a masculine symbol associated with the east where it rises. In ancient Egypt, the mystical blood of Isis renewed the "dead" Sun after it had set in the western sky, indicating a balance between Father Sky and Mother Earth.

Swastika: Long before its use by Hitler, the swastika established itself as one of humanity's most ancient and universal spiritual symbols. Swastika in the Sanskrit language of India means "so be it" (i.e., Amen) and is found in ancient temples and statues throughout the Eastern world where it represents good fortune and healing. Native Americans also used the swastika to represent the four sacred directions on Mother Earth.

Sword: *(see Knife)*

Thorn: Thorns symbolize potential difficulties and obstacles in our path. Removing thorns from a branch or vine symbolizes overcoming obstacles.

Triangle: Since prehistoric times, the triangle standing on its apex (i.e., pointing downward) has represented the female "Portal of Life," the place where new life emerges from a woman's body. It is found on ancient pottery in virtually all parts of the world. In the East, it is often referred to as the "yoni." A triangle with its apex pointing upward is a male symbol, and in the East, it represents fire, one of the Four Primal Elements. Some people today use it to represent the Trinity of Soul, Spirit, and Body/Nature.

Veil: Veils symbolize the presence of mystery and hidden powers. Unveiling symbolizes revelation, recognition, and initiation.

Water: As an entity having no form or structure, it symbolizes an abundance of possibilities that can manifest. Water also symbolizes the primal origin of all physical reality, the *prima materia.* Water is a symbol of fertility and life itself. Associated with the "flowing of waters" immediately before human birth, water can consecrate new undertakings or new paths. Water is a powerful Yin force.

Wheel: Many ancient people viewed the universe as a great wheel rolling through the sky. The Wheel unites a circle with the idea of movement, coming into form, and passing away. *(see Circle)*

Wood: As an important raw material, wood was originally equated with the *prima materia*. Wood is symbolic of the feminine capacity for giving life, hence the ancient custom of wooden coffins.

Yin and Yang: These are the two complementary, cosmological principles of Taoism. The Yin principle embodies Mother Earth, feminine energy, darkness, intuition, and receptiveness. Yin is *Being*. The Yang principle signifies Father Sky, masculine energy, logic and intellect, brightness, and activity. Yang is *Doing*. We must balance these two principles in our minds, our hearts, and our activities if we are to experience harmony and peace in our lives. The two are equal partners, not competing entities.

Activities to Create Symbolic Expression

When you create rituals to celebrate Mother Earth events or your journey through life, consider the following suggestions to help you accomplish your goals. For example: If you desire to emphasize *balancing* as a part of your ceremony, then bread, orchids, or stars are potential symbol choices. Refer to the symbol listings above to select the particular symbols you feel best express your intentions.

Balancing, stabilizing
- arc
- bread
- cross
- gold
- heart
- house
- orchid
- rock
- square
- stars
- wheel

Beginning, starting
- beans
- bread (breaking)
- candle
- dawn
- door
- egg
- key
- pearl
- rose
- seed

Binding, uniting, unifying
- bread (breaking)
- circle
- cord (tying)
- cross
- cup (lifting)
- ivy
- knot
- rainbow
- ring
- river
- smoke

Blessing, consecrating *(also see next listing)*
- cup (lifting)

- oils
- salt
- smoke

Creating a sacred space
- bell
- candle
- cedar
- circle
- cross
- light
- orchid
- room
- salt
- smoke
- square
- veil

Creating mental clarity
- bell
- book
- crystal
- hat
- light
- mirror
- sieve
- smoke

Ending, completing, finishing
- cord (cutting)
- fire
- fruit
- knife/scissors
- knot

Generating, increasing, nurturing
- almond
- cherry
- container
- cowrie shell
- cup
- egg
- fruit
- lemon

- milk
- pearl
- pomegranate
- rose
- seed
- snake
- spiral
- water
- wood

Gaining wisdom or insights

- almond
- apple
- book
- milk
- mirror
- snake
- stairs
- veil

Giving of ourselves, humbling

- cherry
- hand or foot washing

Healing, promoting health

- oils
- sesame

Loving

- heart
- honey
- ivy
- kiss
- ring

Meditating, reflecting

- almond
- bell
- candle
- cedar
- cross
- crystal
- mirror
- stairs

Overcoming obstacles

- cord
- fire
- key
- knife/scissors
- knot
- lily/lotus
- stairs
- thorn

Promoting good fortune
- bamboo
- corn
- egg
- fish
- Horn of Plenty

Receiving, accepting
- arc
- container
- cup/chalice

Releasing, letting go
- cord, cutting
- fire
- key
- knife/scissors
- knot

Transforming, renewing
- cowrie shell
- door
- fire
- hat
- river
- room
- rose
- seed
- smoke
- snake
- spiral
- stairs
- water

— researched and compiled by John McMurphy

Mother Earth Organizations

— A guide to North American organizations that focus upon intimacy with Mother Earth —

Part One: Spiritual Organizations & Centers
  * Judeo–Christian/Western Traditions
  * Native American Traditions
  * Holistic Traditions

Part Two: Environmental Organizations

.　　.　　.

— EARTH CIRCLE —

Wherever you are, you can join millions of your brothers and sisters from around the world in meditation for Mother Earth. Meditate on Mother Earth's harmony, balance, and creativeness at 4 PM Greenwich Mean Time on the first day of each month. Let's circle Mother Earth with love.

.　　.　　.

Part One: Spiritual Organizations & Centers

• Judeo–Christian/Western Traditions

American Society of the Green Cross is a national Christian (nondenominational) spiritual ecology organization with many local chapters whose motto is "Serving and Keeping Creation." The Society publishes the *Green Cross Newsletter.*

The Green Cross
1017 N. Wahsatch Ave.
Colorado Springs, CO 80903
(719) 635–6177

Angela Center is a nondenominational spiritual retreat and educational center sponsored by the Ursuline Sisters, a Catholic community of women. The Center holds year–round classes and retreats that integrate spirituality, psychology, the arts, and social responsibility—many have eco–spiritual themes. Angela Center is near San Francisco.

Angela Center
535 Angela Dr.
Santa Rosa, CA 95403
(707) 528–8578

Center for Inclusive Community (Canada) is dedicated to the principles of Creation Spirituality (see Friends of Creation Spirituality). The Center sponsors classes, workshops, community renewal activities, and "healing circles" throughout Canada.

Center for Inclusive Community
111 Ashberry Place
Waterloo, ON N2T 1G8
(519) 885–6394

Chinook Learning Center offers year–round workshops and retreats on spiritual ecology with links to the ancient Celtic Christian tradition emphasizing the unity of humanity and Nature.

Chinook Learning Center
P. O. Box 57
Clinton, WA 98236
(206) 221–3153

Earth Ministry is a nondenominational eco-spiritual group affiliated with the Episcopal Church. It offers the Earth Ministry Guild and the Episcopal Church Environmental Stewardship Team to provide assistance to local congregations to help them develop an eco-spiritual program and activities. It also publishes *Earth Letter* newsletter.

Earth Ministry
1305 NE 47th St.
Seattle, WA 98105
(206) 632-2426

Ecology Retreat Centre (Canada) is retreat and educational center near Buffalo, NY and Toronto, ON offering a sacred communal space in which people can reconnect with the Divine Presence in Nature. It is founded upon principles of Creation Spirituality (see next entry). Classes, retreats, and workshops are available.

Ecology Retreat Centre
RR 1
Orangeville, ON L9W 2Y8
(519) 941-4560

Friends of Creation Spirituality is an organization with local Creation Spirituality chapters and groups around the world. Creation Spirituality emphasizes that Divinity permeates and unites everything. CS emphasizes social and ecological justice and draws insights from ancient and modern spiritual wisdom from many different cultures, as well as from contemporary science. Matthew Fox, author of many books on CS themes, and other FOCS speakers present programs worldwide. It also publishes the highly recommended *Creation Spirituality* magazine. Each issue of the magazine lists the local CS chapters and networking contacts in most cities in Canada and the U. S. where many workshops and programs are available.

Friends of Creation Spirituality
P. O. Box 19216
Oakland, CA 94619
(510) 482–4894

National Religious Partnership for the Environment unites Protestant, Catholic, and Jewish organizations. Its focus is to aid local congregations in developing eco–spiritual programs and worship activities. It publishes the *Directory of Environmental Activities and Resources in the North American Religious Community.*

National Religious Partnership
1047 Amsterdam Ave.
New York, NY 10025
(212) 316–7441

New Thought Religions: Divine Science, Religious Science/Science of Mind, and Unity Churches New Thought Religions (new applications of Eternal Truth) draw inspiration from many sources, including the spiritual ideas of Ralph Waldo Emerson who emphasized the Divine Unity in Nature. These spiritual groups offer both traditional and innovative worship opportunities, classes, workshops, and support groups which recognize the Oneness of Life and the presence of God in Nature. Consult your telephone directory for churches in your area or contact the respective national headquarters at the addresses below:

DIVINE SCIENCE
1400 Williams Street
Denver, CO 80218
(303) 322–7738

RELIGIOUS SCIENCE INTERNATIONAL
1636 W. First Ave.
Spokane, WA 99204
(509) 624–7000

UNITED CHURCH OF RELIGIOUS SCIENCE
P. O. Box 75127
Los Angeles, CA 90075
(213) 388–2181

ASSOCIATION OF UNITY CHURCHES
P. O. Box 610
Lee's Summit, MO 64063
(816) 524–7414

Quaker/Religious Society of Friends emphasizes the interconnectedness of life on Earth and ways to eliminate violence towards each other and towards all forms of life. The Society publishes *EarthLight*, a quarterly journal of ideas and activities.

EarthLight
Religious Society of Friends
1558 Mercy St.
Mountain View, CA 94041
(415) 960–1767

Shomrei Adamah/Keepers of the Earth is an Eco–spiritual organization drawing upon Jewish tradition. It publishes *Voice of the Trees* newsletter and several books on eco–spiritual topics. There are local chapters.

Shomrei Adamah
5500 Wissahickon Ave. Suite 804C
Philadelphia, PA 19144

Tilikum Center for Retreats and Outdoor Ministry is affiliated with George Fox College (Quaker). The Tilikum Center (*Tilikum* means "friend" in the Chinook language) is an ecumenical outdoor ministry offering workshops, retreats, and Elderhostels. Scripture and sacred verse from different religions are applied to various areas of gardening and horticulture.

Tilikum Center
15321 NE N. Valley Road
Newberg, OR
(503) 538–2763

Wilderness Manna is a Christian nondenominational eco–spiritual ministry seeking to unite Bible Nature Wisdom with environmental science. It publishes two journals: *Churches in Communion with Creation* to aid local churches' eco–spiritual ministries and *Christians in Communion with Nature* which is an eco–spiritual journal for individuals.

Wilderness Manna
P. O. Box 3246
Oakland, CA 94609
(510) 528–1942

• Native American Traditions

Bear Tribe was founded by Sun Bear, an Ojibwa descendent. The Bear Tribe is a self–reliant community dedicated to helping all people open their eyes and ears to Mother Earth and the lessons she can share with us. Workshops, medicine wheel gatherings, and vision quests are presented in the

Bear Tribe community and in other locations. It publishes books and the journal *Wildfire*.

Bear Tribe
P. O. Box 9167
Spokane, WA 99209
(509) 258–7755

Native American Rights Fund seeks to protect the way of life practiced by Native Americans, a lifestyle that is harmonious with Mother Earth. NARF also is fighting several legal battles to protect Native American sacred sites which are being threatened by land developers. A newsletter and educational materials are available.

Native American Rights Fund
1506 Broadway
Boulder, CO 80302
(303) 447–8760

South and Meso American Information Center provides information, materials, and activities focusing upon the indigenous peoples of South and Meso America.

South and Meso American Information Center
P. O. Box 28703
Oakland, CA 94604–8703

• Holistic Spiritual Traditions

Colorado Sacred Earth Institute offers programs and conferences with eco–spiritual themes.

Colorado Sacred Earth Institute
1120 Pine Street
Boulder, CO 80302
(303) 444–0373

Full Circle Center for Holistic Studies offers summer–only workshops at the Cranbrook Educational and Arts Community. Its programs teach the interrelatedness of the spiritual, psychological, physical, ecological, and creative aspects of life.

> Full Circle Center for Holistic Studies
> 13322 Talbot
> Huntington Woods, MI 48070
> (810) 541–3033

Green Pastures Estates is a New England center for spiritual growth and renewal offering year–round workshops honoring Mother Earth's sacredness.

> Green Pastures Estates
> Ladd's Lane
> Epping, NH 03042
> (603) 679–8149

High Winds Association Learning/Retreat Center offers diverse programs, several of which are co–sponsored with the University of Wisconsin. Some are practical—solar design and construction—and others focus upon the sacredness of Mother Earth and planetary healing. It publishes a semi–annual journal and books related to these themes.

> High Winds Assoc. Learning/Retreat Center
> W7136 County Road U
> Plymouth, WI 53073
> (414) 528–7212

Hollyhock (Canada) is an educational center on Cortes Island near Vancouver offering programs on eco-spiritual and spiritual development topics and has a resident naturalist for leading walks and providing insights into native fauna and flora.

Hollyhock
Box 127, Mansions Landing
Cortes Island, B. C. V0P 1K0
(604) 935–6533

Ishpiming Educational Retreat Center is an educational and retreat center calling itself the "Sedona of the Midwest," because it is located near a Mother Earth energy vortex. It offers eco–spiritual classes, workshops, and retreat activities.

Ishpiming Educational Retreat Center:
P. O. Box 340
Manitowish, WI 54545
(715) 686–2372

Oasis Center is a Chicago educational center that offers many workshops and seminars honoring the sacredness of Mother Earth and opportunities for spiritual growth.

Oasis Center
7463 N. Sheridan Road
Chicago, IL 60626
(312) 274–6777

Omega Institute offers eco–spiritual workshops and educational trips to sacred sites around the world.

Omega Institute
260 Lake Drive
Rhinebeck, NY 12572
(914) 266–4444

Peace Place is a spiritual center in Eugene, Oregon offering a holistic view of peace and intimacy with Mother Earth that begins with everyday activities such as preparing and eating food. It offers *The Peaceful Cook*, a cookbook celebrating the natural beauty of food with recipes, suggestions, and poetry for both our own and our planet's health. Also available is *Sol Food*, a solar cook book with recipes and suggestions. Harriet Kofalk, co–author of this book, is the founder of Peace Place.

Peace Place
175 E. 31st
Eugene, OR 97405
(503) 343–5252

Rune Hill Earth Awareness Center offers many workshops and retreat activities to help people connect with Mother Earth. Activities include Nature awareness, communicating with spiritual energy in Nature, and Mother Earth festivals.

Rune Hill Earth Awareness Center
413 Halsey Road
Spencer, NY 14883
(607) 589–6392

Part Two: Environmental Organizations

In addition to highly visible organizations such as the Sierra Club, Green Peace, and the National Wildlife Federation, the following organizations are among many others seeking a way of life in harmony with Mother Earth.

Earthstewards Network is a global grass–roots network of people who work for the healing of Mother Earth and ourselves. The network emphasizes environmental awareness, conflict resolution skills, and citizen diplomacy. Publications include books, a newsletter, and a networking directory.

Earthstewards Network
P. O. Box 10697
Bainbridge Island, WA 98110
(206) 842–7986

The Environmental Exchange is a nonprofit center providing environmental, spiritual, business, and governmental groups with information on using environmental initiatives in their own areas.

The Environmental Exchange
1718 Connecticut Ave. NW
Washington, DC 20009
(202) 387–2182

International Society for Ecology and Culture focuses upon sustainable environmental programs such as the Ladakh Project which draws upon wisdom from the Ladakh culture in Tibet where people nurture intimacy with Mother Earth.

International Society for Ecology and Culture
P. O. Box 9475
Berkeley, CA 94709
(510) 527–3873

Institute for Earth Education is an organization for teachers interested in the environment. It conducts workshops, forums, and conferences and has a journal for teaching environmental awareness.

Institute for Earth Education
Cedar Cove
Greenville, WV 24945
(304) 832–6404

Planet Drum Foundation is a nonprofit membership organization working to promote sustainable resources and living in harmony with Mother

Earth. It publishes a newsletter *Raise the Stakes* and offers networking services.

Planet Drum Foundation
P. O. Box 31251
San Francisco, CA 94131
(415) 285–6556

University of Global Education is a United Nations non–governmental organization for promoting intimacy with Mother Earth. It offers Project NatureConnect with materials for guided home study in applied eco–psychology, global communication networks, and books including *Connecting with Nature* by Michael J. Cohen.

University of Global Education
P. O. Box 12072
Portland, OR 97212
(503) 288–5846

— Last Minute Items —

North American Coalition on Religion and the Environment is an organization helping religious groups develop eco–spiritual programs.

NACRE
5 Thomas Circle
Washington, DC 20005
(202) 462–2591

Note: Harriet and John are avid networkers and continue to find eco–spiritual groups in all parts of the planet. For updates on these organizations, please contact them through Amaranth Publishing at the address on the inside title page.

— John McMurphy and Harriet Kofalk

About the Authors

Jeff Davis is an award–winning writer whose poetry and short stories have appeared in national literary journals. He also teaches college and high school humanities and literature courses in the Dallas area.

Harriet Kofalk is the founder of Peace Place, a center for spiritual growth, in Eugene, Oregon. She has written two books: *The Peaceful Cook* and *Sol Food*. Her poetry regularly appears in *Talking Leaves*, an eco–spiritual journal. Her poetry also appears in the book *Earth Prayers*.

Amy Martin is a writer whose essays have appeared in the environmental journal *Garbage, The Dallas Morning News, The Dallas Times Herald*, and on KERA, National Public Radio for Dallas–Fort Worth. She also creates and leads rituals and ceremonies honoring Mother Earth.

John McMurphy, Ph.D. teaches adult seminars in mythology at the University of Texas, Southern Methodist University, Texas Christian University and in spiritual centers across the U. S. and Canada. His other books are *Secrets from Great Minds* and *Living Deliberately*. He founded The Walden Institute, an educational organization in Dallas inspired by the works of Thoreau and Emerson.

·   ·   ·

Note: You may notice that this book has a small departure from the traditional book layout. In most books, publishers include blank pages for stylistic concerns such as having each chapter start on a right–hand page. We had a choice about including blank pages for this stylistic concern. We chose not to include them, however, because a few blank pages placed in several thousand books would consume a great deal of paper and energy. We feel that conserving Mother Earth's resources is a greater concern than the concern for stylistic appearance. We believe this small break from the traditional book layout will not affect the book's readability or your enjoyment of our work. As we emphasize throughout this book, each of us can become more mindful of Mother Earth when we make decisions.